WINGS
OVER THE GULF

Shirley Kay

GW00578090

Published with
the support and
encouragement of

AIR BP

MOTIVATE
PUBLISHING

Published by **Motivate Publishing**

PO Box 2331, Dubai, UAE. Tel: (04) 824060, Fax: (04) 824436.
PO Box 43072, Abu Dhabi, UAE. Tel: (02) 311666, Fax: (02) 311888.
London House, 19 Old Court Place, Kensington High Street, London W8 4PL.
Tel: (0171) 938 2222, Fax: (0171) 937 7293.

Directors: Obaid Humaid Al Tayer and Ian Fairservice.

First published 1995.
© 1995 Shirley Kay and Motivate Publishing.

ISBN 1 873544 63 4

British Library Cataloguing-in-Publication Data. A catalogue record for this book is available from the British Library.

Printed by Emirates Printing Press, Dubai.

Front cover: *Over Dubai Creek, 1951*
Title page: *A Spaf Pioneer*
This page: *The Lockheed F117 Stealth fighter*
Back cover: *The world's most advanced aircraft at the Dubai air show*

CONTENTS

INTRODUCTION

The Gulf became a major route for aeroplanes very early on in the history of aviation. It was, indeed, part of the longest air route in the world, a service carrying passengers and mail some 13,000 miles from London to Australia. The service depended on numerous landing grounds all along the Arab shores of the Gulf, landing grounds which have given rise to the large modern airports of today.

The first aeroplane, flown in America less than a hundred years ago, was closer to a microlight than a plane, and flew a few hundred yards at a time. Soon planes could fly a few miles, or tens of miles, but many hundreds of miles was a different challenge. Nevertheless, just 15 years after the first plane had been flown, British pilots headed for India in the flimsy, double-winged, fabric-covered biplanes left over from World War I. Their zigzag route ran via Cairo and Baghdad, then along the Persian shores of the Gulf to Karachi, with stopping places at frequent intervals along the way.

A dozen years later the route was shifted to the southern side of the Gulf: Kuwait, Bahrain, and Sharjah were suddenly connected by regular air services to the world at large. It was a decisive move in opening the doors to trade and travel, which in the last decade of the century have brought millions of passengers each year to the airports of the Gulf states. Alongside the commercial flights, smaller planes were carrying other travellers; the geophysicists and personnel of oil companies prospecting in the deserts throughout the Gulf. Far faster military jets also took off from these same airfields and many others, to patrol the skies of the Gulf. Their mission culminated in the first great conflict fought primarily in the air, in 1991 for the liberation of Kuwait.

Today aviation of all kinds is of primary interest to the inhabitants of the Gulf. The world's third largest air show has become established in Dubai as a biennial market place for the most modern commercial and military aircraft, whose purchasers now are the local airlines and air forces of the Gulf states themselves.

A landing strip at Umm al Zamul, the point where Saudi Arabia, Oman and the UAE meet.

PRELUDE: TAKE-OFF

Man has always dreamed of following the birds into the sky, as ancient legends show. The 3,000-year-old Greek story of Icarus tells how he and his father tried to escape imprisonment on the island of Crete by flying away. Equipped with wings of feathers fixed to his arms with wax, he soared higher, ever higher . . . until he came too close to the sun, the wax melted, and he crashed into the sea. All too many of the pioneers of flight were to follow his fate.

At the start of the 20th century the dream of controlled flight finally became a reality. In 1903, two remarkably gifted American brothers, Wilbur and Orville Wright, at last managed to fly a powered, controllable machine into the air. A century of development, based on this first flight, has made flying now an everyday method of travel.

The Wrights were not, however, the first men to rise into the air. For more than a hundred years this had been possible, ever since the first hydrogen balloon went up over Paris in 1783. That balloon was not manned and when it came down in a village some miles away, the villagers took it for a dragon and hacked it to pieces. A month later the Montgolfier brothers flew a hot-air balloon with a crew of animals, and later in the same year two bold young Frenchmen took off in the hot-air balloon. By the end of that century, men had risen almost five miles up into the atmosphere, carried by balloons.

But balloons had a few serious disadvantages. They could only go where the wind took them, and they were very susceptible to fires. Of the flying machines which followed them, the great hydrogen-

The 'Wright Flyer' takes off on the world's first ever plane flight, December 1903. Orville Wright pilots it, lying across the lower wing, Wilbur stands on the right.

7

filled airships, while powered and controllable, suffered even more spectacular fires, and winged gliders, developed at the very end of the 19th century, were completely at the mercy of the winds.

A cross between the two – a powered, controllable winged plane – became the dream of the Wright brothers. These two sons of an American bishop were inseparable friends, they worked together and both still lived at home with their parents. At the turn of the century they were around 30 years old, and ran a company manufacturing bicycles, the 'Wright specials'. All their spare time, however, was spent reading about aerodynamics, and observing in minute detail the flight of birds.

The Flyer

They built kites, then gliders, to observe the effects of what they had studied. They obtained meteorological reports to help select a site to fly them. Eventually they chose a great stretch of sand dunes close to the Atlantic at Kitty Hawk. There, each autumn for four years, they flew and adjusted their models, gradually perfecting their ability to control and turn a winged plane.

The key to their success came from the flight of birds. The Wrights saw that wings must twist slightly in making a turn. They called it 'wing-warping', and achieved the same effect in their models by means of lines running inwards from the ends of the wings. This enabled them to control the lateral balance of their gliders, as ailerons do today.

By December 1903 their careful experiments over four years had prepared them for their first powered flight. They brought their novel flying machine, the Wright Flyer, to the top of their ramp, and helped by local fishermen, Orville launched off. A wooden framed biplane, its double wings covered with fabric, it stood on sled-type runners. Orville lay down across the lower wing, which also carried a small motor driving two propellers facing backwards. He did not get far, staying up just 12 seconds. But the Wrights patiently adjusted, adapted, tried again, and on their fourth flight of the day Wilbur stayed up for nearly a minute and travelled 284 yards. One of their fishermen helpers took photographs of these epic experiments for them.

They had found the key to manned flight but they were not showmen and they had firm ideas as to the use of their invention, on which they took out a patent. They saw their machines as a means of military reconnaissance, perhaps later carrying mail and even passengers. It was several years before their lead was followed, but by 1908 they began to give licences for others to build their Flyers. One of their early customers was Eustace Short, who was to found Short Brothers (another of the fruitful brother partnerships in aviation), the first aircraft manufacturers in the world. Their flying boats, some years later, would be vital to air transport in the Gulf.

The following year the sea was crossed: a Frenchman, Louis Blériot, made the first daring flight from Calais to Dover. A copy of Bleriot's plane was bought the next year, 1910, by Charles Ritchie, a young engineer of the Anglo-Persian Oil Company (now BP). He wanted it for surveying pipeline routes in Persia, and assembled the aircraft

Louis Blériot takes off to cross the Channel in 1909.

A Handley Page V/1500, Britain's largest World War I bomber, produced at the end of the war to bomb Germany from England, but too late for wartime service.

on the spot. He read the instruction book, and with no further knowledge of flying took off from a desert strip. It was the first flight made in the Middle East, but was not a long one. The plane crashed upside down in a gulley; Ritchie emerged unhurt.

Three years later, in 1913, a French pilot flew 2,500 miles from Paris to Cairo, with numerous stops on the way of course. It was a foretaste of things to come; a possibility of air routes stretching ever eastwards. But Europe was on the eve of a disaster which would cast flying in a quite different light.

World War I

When World War I started in 1914, man had been able to fly winged planes for a mere decade. At first there had been little enthusiasm in the armed forces for planes; the British military had complained that they would frighten the horses. By 1914, however, their use for reconnaissance and aerial photography was appreciated, but their real military potential was not recognised. Nevertheless, the countries of Europe had

amassed some warplanes: Germany had 240, France 150 and Britain barely 100.

The war was to advance the new technology of flight more than any equivalent period of peace would ever have done. Quite soon the opposing armies, who controlled the planes, realised that they could be used for attack as well as reconnaissance. One hurdle had to be overcome. A machine gun firing forwards unfortunately shot off the propeller. Once an interrupter system, allowing the gun to fire only between the blades of the propeller, was invented, fighter planes came into their own and production raced ahead. Bomber planes were also developed from an early version in which the pilot simply threw his small bomb over the side of the open cockpit.

By the end of the war, Britain alone had 22,500 aircraft and the only independent air force in the world. Initially flying was an attribute of the army and navy, each of which had their own Royal Flying Corps, but in 1918 the Royal Air Force was founded as an autonomous body. It was a force, however, whose future did not look particularly rosy.

THE PIONEERS

At the end of World War I, Europe was overstocked with redundant planes and pilots. The RAF cut down its squadrons (fighting units of 12 planes each) from 188 to a mere 33, of which six were to be sent to India. Considerable technical advances had been made in airplane design, but the boundaries of flying had not extended beyond the wartime battle fields, and the United States. Now was the time for adventurous pilots, spurred on by the offer of huge cash prizes, to push those boundaries outwards.

In 1919 the Atlantic was crossed for the first time, from Newfoundland to Ireland in 16½ hours, by Captain John Alcock and Lieutenant Arthur Brown. They flew a Vickers Vimy, a twin-engined bomber produced at the end of the war, stripped out and carrying 865 gallons of fuel against a normal 516 gallons. This versatile, snub-nosed biplane had been designed to bomb Berlin, but came into production just too late for wartime service. The Vimy had a huge wingspan of 68 feet and was 43½ feet long. Its wooden frame was covered with hand-sewn cotton fabric and it was powered by twin Rolls-Royce engines.

To the East

In the same year, the Australian Prime Minister offered a prize of £10,000 for the first flight from England to Australia completed in less than 30 days. Two Australian pilots, brothers Captain Ross and Lieutenant Keith Smith, took up the challenge. Ross Smith had become an ace pilot with the Australian Flying Squadron in Egypt and Palestine,

A replica of the Vickers Vimy bomber first produced at the end of World War I. This replica was flown from England to Australia in 1994.

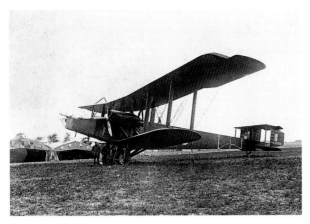

The Handley Page 0/400 flown by Ross Smith in the First World War in Palestine and Jordan, and then to India.

flying for General Allenby and Lawrence of Arabia. In November 1918, he had already flown a Handley Page 0/400 twin-engined bomber from Cairo to India, along the Persian coast of the Gulf, with Major General Borton and Major General Salmond, RAF commander in the Middle East. Theirs was the first plane to make the journey; it was followed five weeks later from England to India by a larger Handley Page four-engined V/1500, another end-of-the-war bomber.

Ross Smith and Borton continued eastwards from India by ship, to survey landing grounds for a possible air route to Australia. They intended to dump 200 gallons of petrol at every possible landing ground on the way, but lost their fuel when the ship caught fire. Ross was back in India by mid-1919 when he heard of the prize, which must be collected by the end of that year.

He chose his brother as navigator and co-pilot, and mechanics Jim Bennett and Wally Shiers, who had served with him in the Middle East and on the flight to India. They were expert and versatile; at Cairo, Shiers successfully repaired a cracked induction pipe with chewing gum. Borton obtained for them a Vickers Vimy (the reserve plane built for Alcock and Brown), which was also fitted with an extra fuel tank. A large quantity of fuel was so precious for the journey that the crew of four restricted themselves to a toothbrush each, by way of luggage. Ross also refused a radio for reasons of weight; anyway calling for help would be of little use where he was going.

They set out in terrible weather in early November; so cold was it on the first stage to Lyons that their sandwiches froze solid (planes had no heating in those days, and the cockpits were open), they were covered in snow and their

Ross and Keith Smith with mechanics Jim Bennett and Wally Shiers, and the Vickers Vimy they flew from England to Australia in 1919.

Ross Smith, Australian World War I ace pilot and the first to fly from England to Australia. He died in a plane crash in 1922.

goggles iced over. The weather did not improve quickly; at Ramadie in Iraq, where they stopped overnight, the winds became so violent that a crowd of helpers had to hold the plane down all night. It was not until they flew south through India that they needed their tropical sun helmets.

The brothers had hoped to fly 600 miles a day, but often they made less than half that distance. Against strong headwinds the Vimy's speed could drop as low as 20 mph. The engines were so noisy that they could not hear each other speak and Ross was deaf for a while when they reached India. The plane was so heavy to fly that the pilot had to keep both hands gripping the wheel and both feet on the rudders all the time. Altogether, it took them 28 arduous days to reach Australia, but one of their best sections was through the Gulf where Ross had flown before; they stopped only at Basra, Bandar Abbas and Karachi to refuel, the longest stages of the whole flight. Ross commented on the fantastic colours of the rugged and wonderful desert scenery along the Gulf.

The Smith brothers were knighted for their efforts, and Ross wrote accounts of the epic flight for the *National Geographic*, and in a book. But success was short lived. Like all too many early aviators, he and Jim Bennett were killed three years later in a single engined amphibious

Vickers Viking which they were testing for a flight around the world. Keith should have been with them on the test flight but his train was late; he arrived just in time to see the plane hit the ground and was first to reach the wreck. Some two years earlier, John Alcock had also died in the crash of a similar Viking.

In autumn of 1994, just 75 years after the Smith brothers' flight, two adventurous modern pilots retraced their route in a replica of the Vickers Vimy that they had flown. This latter-day Vimy followed the Arabian shore of the Gulf, stopping at Bahrain and Muscat. The plane benefited from such modern amenities as radios and navigational equipment (to appease air-traffic controllers) and was accompanied by a support team; even so, they took two weeks longer to reach Australia than the Smith brothers had done.

Air mail

In 1919, however, the RAF itself was still in search of a role, and that would only be provided at the Cairo Conference of 1920. Winston Churchill, then Colonial Secretary, proposed that the RAF should be responsible for the security of Transjordan and Mesopotamia (Jordan and Iraq to use their present names), for which Britain held the Mandate. The Army opposed the plan furiously. They had over 100,000 British and Indian troops in Iraq alone, who would be replaced by a mere eight RAF squadrons with a small military back-up. But Churchill insisted. The RAF would be unobtrusive, based on airstrips out in the desert, but when called upon, its intervention in a desert environment would be lethal. The argument that carried the day, however, was economic. Using the RAF, the cost to the British government dropped from £20 million a year to below £4 million, and down again to a little over £1 million by 1929 when the military back-up, no longer needed, was withdrawn.

The Middle East was the saving of the RAF. Here they had a wider role. They were immediately asked to establish an air mail service from Cairo to Baghdad. This was a route over desolate terrain, and the RAF pilots flew with few instruments and no radio. Searching for lost planes would be expensive. So they marked the route, from Amman through almost to Baghdad, by painting a white stripe across the black lava of southern Syria, and ploughing a furrow for 470 miles across the sands beyond. The pilots came to

The hazards of early flying. A KLM mail plane lies crashed in the Jordan desert.

know the route as 'flying the furrow'.

In case of trouble (not infrequent, with early planes carrying limited fuel supplies), an emergency landing strip was cleared and marked out every 25 miles along the route. At each landing strip was a fuel supply, usually buried under the sand. The fuel itself was of no interest to the bedouin in that pre-pick-up truck era, but oil drums were at a premium in desert culture. Arrows beside the furrow marked the approach of these strips.

The presence of an RAF team at one of these airstrips almost brought disaster to a bedouin leader described by T. E. Lawrence as "the greatest fighting man in northern Arabia". Sheikh Audah and his men had ridden from Ma'an in Jordan up into Iraq to raid the camels of tribes there. They were spotted and beat a hasty retreat; to survive the journey home they needed to fill their water bags at Rutbah wells, deep in the desert of western Iraq. Some RAF men were at the airstrip there at the time; when the bedouin saw them near the wells they rode on, taking them for Iraqi government troops sent to catch them. The terrible ride home without water cost many of Audah's followers their lives. The RAF men knew nothing of the tragedy; they more often tried to save the lives of sick

bedouin on their route by flying them to hospital.

By 1921 the route was ready and the air mail service began. Along the air mail route the RAF flew Vickers Vimy bombers, and from 1922 onwards they had another Vickers biplane, the Vernon. A further former warplane, the de Havilland DH9A, was specially adapted for use in the Middle East. These planes were given a spare wheel, a spare tropical radiator, two auxiliary fuel tanks under the top mainplane, and they carried five-gallon drums of drinking water on their bomb racks. Weight was always a problem for early planes flying over the desert; the amount of fuel carried must be balanced against water supplies and the load of mail.

All the planes flown in this period were biplanes, their huge double wings making them reminiscent of box kites. They were built with a wooden frame over which fabric was tightly stretched and then painted. For many years the British clung to their biplanes, long after the Americans had moved on to smooth, swift monoplanes far closer to the planes of today. There was even resistance to accepting the superiority of metal over wood. This was put to the test when an RAF team of four flying boats set out for Australia in 1927: two of them were fitted with new metal propellers, two kept to the traditional wooden ones. By the time they reached Karachi, after flying along the Gulf, they had had so much trouble with the wooden propellers that they scrapped them for the metal ones.

From 1931, however, the RAF were equipped with the hardy two-seater Westland Wapiti biplanes, first ordered for the Australian air force. These planes were descendants of the DH9As but built now all of metal. However the specification was to use as many of the DH9A parts as possible, for reasons of economy. The Wapitis had a maximum speed of 135 mph and could cruise at 110. Their range was 530 miles and they were used extensively by the RAF in Iraq, the Gulf and India. Pilots' equipment was improving too by then: in 1929 parachutes became standard issue for the first time (they had never been used in the war because the government thought they would encourage pilots to abandon their planes); aircraft radios and oxygen equipment for the crew were now also supplied. Flying was no longer quite such a launch into the blue.

Blazing the trail

For the first few years, the RAF had the skies of the Middle East to themselves. In 1924, however, Imperial Airways was founded as the British national carrier, aptly named for the role it was to undertake. The government dreamed of commercial flights from Britain to India, and beyond – even as far as Australia. The RAF were instructed to pave the way.

Ever since late in 1918, when the RAF made their first through flights to India, they had flown regularly there. Their route ran from Cairo to Baghdad, then Shaibah near Basra, along the Persian coast of the Gulf via Bushire, Bandar Abbas and Jask, to Gwadar in Baluchistan, and finally Karachi. The north coast of the Gulf offered the shortest route for this section of the already very dog-legged journey which went south across Europe to Alexandria or Cairo, then north-east via Amman to Baghdad, and thence south east to Basra. It was assumed that Imperial Airways would use the landing grounds the RAF had established along the route, including those on the Persian coast, and their service was scheduled to start along that line in 1926. Unfortunately problems with the government of Persia delayed the start of the service. By early 1929, the British began to despair of the Persian coast route and instructed the RAF to survey the Arabian coast instead. Flying boats were thought to be the best aircraft for this shore: "As regards alighting areas, the west side of the Arabian Gulf favours flying boats probably more than any other area over which British flying boats operate" was the verdict after initial surveys.

In March 1929, the RAF's 203 Squadron arrived in the Shatt al Arab, near Basra, with three Supermarine Southampton flying boats. These biplanes carried a crew of five. They had metal hulls of duralumin, which allowed the crews the luxury of smoking on board, and cooking their meals during flight. They carried large water and petrol supplies, but had to dispense with beds for the crew, for reasons of weight. In summer the crew all slept outside, lying on the lower plane of the flying boat; in winter they slept on the floor of the hull, in which conditions were strictly spartan.

From 1931 they were provided with Short Brothers Rangoon flying boats in which living conditions were much better. These planes had two light, airy cabins with beds for the whole crew

De Havilland's World War I DH9A was adapted for Middle East use after the war.

The Westland Wapiti, closely based on the DH9A, was widely used by the RAF in the Middle East.

203 Squadron used Southampton flying boats for their early surveys of the Arabian Gulf shore.

of six. They were based on the design of Short's Calcuttas which had been built for Imperial Airways to use across the Mediterranean, where they carried 15 passengers. Although they were not fast (average cruising speed was about 75 mph), they were strong craft: on one occasion a Rangoon was forced to land out to sea on the way to Gwadar when its fuel pump failed. The crew managed to taxi for eight and a half hours to reach Gwadar. So handy were the crew that several times they succeeded in changing an engine themselves, when they had trouble away from base.

The squadron's task was to find a southern route which could be taken by land aircraft or seaplanes as far as Gwadar, which at the time belonged to Muscat and so was not affected by the Persian problems. They were to select and mark landing grounds, find suitable stretches of sheltered water where seaplanes could alight and fix moorings there, install petrol tanks, arrange for resthouses and set up wireless stations.

In April the squadron flew to Bahrain, where British planes were welcomed by the Sheikh who foresaw an increase in commerce. They took Sheikh Hamad for a flight, to visit the Sheikh of Qatar, causing quite a stir on their arrival at Doha. In May· they returned to mark out a landing ground near the Sheikh's palace in Manama, acknowledging that it was not ideal but hoping it would do at least for

RAF planes en route to India. They inspected a much better area on Muharraq island, but rejected it because of the difficulty of transporting passengers from one island to the other.

Between the two islands, in Khor Khaliya, they found an excellent alighting area for flying boats and set up moorings, just opposite a resthouse which they had acquired in the old quarantine station. Then they flew on down to Muscat.

The landscape in Muscat was less ideally adapted to flying than that of Bahrain, but the Sultan and his people were helpful and the RAF team quickly found a house in the town which could serve as resthouse and wireless station. They surveyed the mountainous terrain within easy reach of Muscat and came to the conclusion that the only usable flat land was in the valley of Bait al Falaj, just inland of Muttrah. Here they cleared and marked a landing strip, hoping it would suffice for the occasional flights they thought would use it.

An alighting area for flying boats was also difficult to find. Muscat Cove provided a beautifully sheltered mooring area, but planes could not land or take off there because of the rocky peaks around the bay. They would have to land on the open sea and taxi into the moorings laid near the coaling station within the cove.

The team then flew southwards along the coast

to the most easterly tip of Oman, Ras al Hadd, where they found the best stretch of water for flying boats, and an excellent landing ground which had already been marked out by RAF crews from Aden.

In August of 1929, one of their flying boats visited Ras al Khaimah, then flew on to Abu Dhabi where they were hospitably entertained by Sheikh Shakhbut. His return visit to their aircraft was made in rough seas; as his boat came alongside, the lower wing of the plane was holed. 203 Squadron's officer asked that the Sheikh should "be officially thanked for (his) hospitality", and that it should "be explained that the covering of an aeroplane is more fragile than it appears".

By 1930 the facilities set up by 203 Squadron were already in regular use by the RAF. Only a middle station was lacking, somewhere safe to land between Bahrain and Muscat. The squadron flew over every village, town, hamlet and creek, in their search for a suitable place. This was little known territory to westerners for none had ever lived there, and as one RAF man put it: "the existing maps are largely printed imagination".

The RAF had already had a glimpse of the peninsula which is now the United Arab Emirates. An RAF team had carried out a brief survey of the coast from naval ships in the mid-1920s, and a closer look had been taken by an intrepid team of four, who rode over it on camels. They landed in Sohar in autumn of 1927 and set off up the Wadi Jizi with an armed guard of some 60 local tribesmen. As they moved into the interior the going became more difficult. They were refused entry to Buraimi oasis which they needed to cross in order to get to Abu Dhabi, their goal. They camped in Mahdah and, after fruitless negotiations, set off for Sharjah. It was a tough trek through driving sand, excessive heat and with only brackish water to drink. The interior, they concluded, was not suitable for a landing ground.

The diligent 203 Squadron checked their findings from the air. In 1930 two of the flying boats flew from Abu Dhabi direct to Sohar, where they had already set up an emergency airstrip. They reported afterwards that "it was a most interesting flight, though a somewhat anxious one, as a good deal of the country seemed quite unsuitable for even a land aircraft to alight on."

The coast would be the better solution, but for flying boats the open sea there was ruled out because "the prevailing north-west wind causes a long swell to roll up on the Trucial Coast" (as the United Arab Emirates was then called). By the time 203 Squadron arrived, the RAF had decided that Ras al Khaimah would be the ideal place. It

Muscat Bay offered sheltered moorings, but flying boats first had to land on the open sea and taxi in.

An officer of 203 Squadron being entertained by Abu Dhabi sheikhs in 1929.

had an excellent creek for flying boats, level land for a landing ground just inland of the creek, and was the nearest feasible point to Gwadar on the Baluchi coast. North of Ras al Khaimah, the mountains of Musandam rose straight from the sea, a daunting terrain inhabited by the fierce Shihuh tribes.

Negotiations

The squadron flew down to Ras al Khaimah bringing Britain's senior diplomatic representative in the Gulf, the Political Resident, with them. The negotiations were not successful. Sheikh Sultan bin Salim was willing to allow the RAF to fly through, but he foresaw that civil planes would mean foreigners in his town, where none had lived before.

After a year of protracted negotiations, the British decided to put a fuel barge in the creek anyway. The Anglo-Persian Oil Company (which later became BP) towed a barge down from Basra, and a navy sloop brought it into Ras al Khaimah. The RAF brought the Political Resident along to watch the arrival of the barge and continue negotiations, but that night the Shihuh staged an impressive wardance on the shores of the creek.

The RAF began to look elsewhere.

Dubai creek was their next choice for a flying boat alighting ground, and Sheikh Saeed was in favour, for he saw the commercial benefit. But he had yet to convince his relatives when he fell seriously ill, and negotiations were postponed. Abu Dhabi had sheltered water and suitable flat land but was too far from Gwadar for a plane to make it in one hop. Nevertheless, planes would have to fly along the Abu Dhabi coast, since it would be safer than crossing the open sea, so the RAF cleared a landing strip on the remote Bani Yas island and installed a fuel tank there.

Imperial Airways announced early in 1932 that they could fly land planes along the route, and the RAF switched their efforts to finding landing grounds. They surveyed Kalba, Dibba and Sharjah. They would have preferred the east coast, since it was closer to Gwadar, but Dibba had no suitable flat ground and was surrounded by mountains, and at Kalba the beach was not good for landing equipment, fuel and stores.

Sharjah became their first choice, and this time negotiations were successful. Agreement for an airport was concluded in July 1932 and the Arabian route was in place. The mission of 203 Squadron in the region was all but completed.

DH9As over the Jordan Valley in the 1920s.

Les Vowles
04

IMPERIAL AIRWAYS

Civil aviation came into being immediately after World War I, when two Handley Page bombers were converted to carry passengers from England to France. In the next few years numerous fledgling airlines were launched throughout Europe and competition became very fierce. The first British airline, Aircraft Transport and Travel Ltd, transported passengers and mail on two routes, London-Paris and London-Brussels, just like the Channel Tunnel would do in the last decade of the century. But also like the tunnel, they initially found it difficult to make their operations pay.

In the next year or two, several companies were founded, and the original one was absorbed, but all floundered in the face of competition from European airlines which received large government subsidies. The British government gave the English lines small subsidies, but soon realised that in fact, by subsidising each one, it was simply competing against itself. It urged the four surviving British companies (Handley Page Transport, Instone, Daimler Airway, British Marine Air Navigation) to sink their rivalry and merge in one large monopoly company with £1 million capital and £1 million government subsidy to be paid over 10 years.

In 1924 the companies finally agreed terms and pooled their 15 existing aircraft. Imperial Airways was launched as 'the chosen instrument of the government'. In case of national emergency, the government reserved the right to take over all the company's aircraft and equipment, but government financing assured a firm start for the airline. It was the start of a long life also, for Imperial Airways eventually became British Overseas Airways

Imperial Airways used de Havilland's DH66 Hercules planes on their original route to India, via Egypt and Iraq, then along the Persian coast.

Corporation and finally the British Airways of today.

In the beginning, however, all was not plain sailing. Competition in Europe was still intense and the subsidy would not last forever. The government directed the young airline to look to empire routes, and live up to its name. The route to India, naturally, should be the first. The RAF, who had already pioneered these routes, would lend a hand.

From Croydon

The airport from which these ambitious flights were to be launched was Croydon, in south London. Converted from an RAF base in 1920, this was the world's first custom-built passenger airport and offered the latest in control systems. Aircraft were signalled for take-off by a man with a red flag; there was a control tower, a first-ever air traffic controller, a wireless telegraph operator, and by 1930 a powerful flashing beacon to guide planes in, red neon lights marking the landing area, and a bad-weather landing aid.

The passengers gathered in the airport building were dressed for the adventurous journey they were about to undertake, the men wearing sun helmets, the ladies with hats, white gloves and cotton dresses. It must have been something of an anticlimax to find that they flew only as far as Basle or Paris before leaving the plane and boarding a train. Imperial Airways met endless problems establishing the European section of the route. The Alps were too high to fly over, and they never seemed to get overflying rights from all the countries along the way at the same time. It was not until 1938 that the European stage of the journey became completely airborne.

Means of travel on this route were varied if nothing else. In Brindisi, Genoa, Salonika or Athens passengers boarded a flying boat for the journey across the Mediterranean to Tripoli (Libya), Alexandria, or Galilee. The precise route varied from year to year, as negotiations with the various countries flourished or failed. From the southern shore of the Mediterranean on, a land plane took over again.

Across the desert

At the end of 1926 Imperial Airways inherited the RAF mail route from Cairo to Baghdad, as part of the route to India. They were also inheriting use of all the RAF landing strips along the way; in fact the RAF had paved the way. On December 27 1926, with great ceremony, the Secretary of State for Air, Sir Samuel Hoare, accompanied by Lady Hoare and a party of VIPs, were flown by Imperial Airways from London to Delhi, where they arrived on January 8 1927. Ordinary passengers were supposed to follow them a few days later, when scheduled flights started on January 1.

Unfortunately the British had just refused permission to a German airline, flying into Teheran, to continue from there to Baghdad. It

Croydon airport in the 1930s. Croydon was the world's first custom-built commercial airport, opened in 1920.

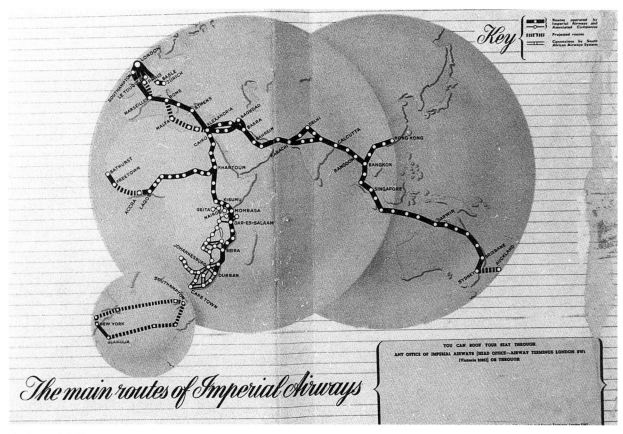

An Imperial Airways route map.

would have been a useful route for the Persians, who were understandably vexed. They delayed permission for Imperial Airways to fly along their southern coast. The grand imperial route was destined to stop abruptly at Basra, until the hitch could be resolved in 1929 and a contract for a three-year use of the route agreed.

Meanwhile Imperial Airways worked on the early sections of their route. They kept to the dog-legged route via Egypt, established by the RAF. Passengers were ferried by train to a harbour on the northern shore of the Mediterranean, then crossed the Mediterranean by flying boat to Alexandria

The DH66 'City of Karachi' stops on the journey to India.

(or Galilee) and thence by land plane, following the RAF's furrow across the deserts of Syria and Iraq, to Baghdad. However, while RAF personnel could rough it in the desert, Imperial Airways' wealthy passengers could not be expected to. They would need a comfortable night's lodging somewhere between Alexandria and Baghdad, for in the 1920s the airline never flew at night.

The choice was limited, to say the least. Imperial Airways picked Rutbah Wells, where at least water was available. It left a lasting impression on their passengers – as one Anglo-Persian oil man wrote in the *Imperial Gazette*: "The spot is unforgettable. Here, in the heart of desertdom, a fort, rather like one of Palmerston's efforts, has been set up succinctly . . .. This neat construction faces four square into a universal vacancy." The fort-cum-resthouse was built around an open courtyard; it was run by British staff, with food and fuel being brought across the desert from Baghdad, 240 miles away.

Imperial's planes were of course carrying quantities of mail as well as passengers. Indeed, mail was to become of increasing importance to the airline. When the route did finally extend to India, in 1929, they carried 50,000 Christmas letters in one week. By the following year they were experimenting with air freight – flowers, fruit and vegetables were flown from Alexandria to London, cotton was taken by air from Egypt to London then on to Manchester, and in the other direction emergency medicines were flown from Paris to Cairo.

In August of 1929 a Gulf pearl merchant chartered one of their planes for the journey from Basra to Bahrain and back. It was the first civil plane to land on the island and the pilot offered joyrides to anyone bold enough to try. He took 68 passengers in turn into the air, but had to disappoint a further couple of hundred because he feared running out of fuel, due to the "lack of petrol on the island".

Persian route

In the spring of 1929 Imperial Airways could at last fly through to India. The *Imperial Gazette* of the time exulted that the journey by plane from London to Karachi took only seven days, compared with 15 days by ship, but added hopefully: "In years to come the journey will be made in three to four days". This journey of almost 5,000 miles was already the longest air route in the world. A ticket to India cost around £120, so large a sum at the time that most passengers were government officials. By the end of 1929, however, Imperial Airways were already negotiating to extend the route from India through to Australia, a total distance from London of some 13,000 miles!

The route along the Persian coast of the Gulf made use of the RAF landing strips at Bushire, Lingeh, Bandar Abbas, Jask and Charbah, before stopping at Gwadar in Baluchistan, which was then Omani territory, followed by Karachi. The main stops on the Persian coast were Bushire and Jask, with the others as refuelling or emergency landing grounds in case of need. The small, three-engined de Havilland 'Hercules' airliners flew just off the coast, offering the passengers a good view of the mountains of Persia. The excitement of the "magic journey" is described in Harry Harper's *The Romance of a Modern Airway*: "On this stage of the flight you pass that Island of Abadan on which are situated the great distilleries of the Anglo-Persian Oil Company . . .. On near swamps, plains and mountains you fly to Bushire . . .. Here you alight and enjoy a meal in the resthouse on the edge of the aerodrome."

At the refuelling stop in Lingeh, passengers had time to appreciate the extreme heat of summer, and

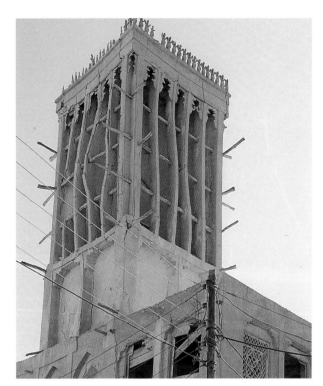

Passengers were amazed by the ingenious wind towers used to cool buildings in Lingeh.

to admire the local architecture: "The houses here are equipped with curious wind towers . . . to catch every breath of cool wind that may blow." Finally, at the end of their journey, they could marvel at the fact that last Saturday morning they were in London, and now, on Friday evening "having voyaged in swift luxury over land and sea", here they were in India.

Already, however, Imperial Airways felt uneasy about this Persian route and asked the RAF to survey the Arabian coast for a possible alternative. Their concern was well founded. When the time came to renew their agreement for the Persian route, the Persian government announced that they must fly by another, inland route instead. This inland route was to run via Isfahan, Kerman, Yazd, Bampur and then on to Gwadar. It was not a route which had been taken by air before, so Imperial Airways sent surveyors to inspect it by land. They were appalled. It would involve crossing mountains over 14,000 feet high, covered in permanent snows, and landing in regions where there were no roads. Emergency landing grounds would be out of the question. The Arabian route seemed more attractive every day.

Ironically, when Imperial Airways ceased to use the Persian route, that government dropped their demand that airlines fly inland and both the Dutch and French airlines were given permission to use the coastal route established by the British instead.

Refuelling the inaugural DH66 with a jerrycan from the upper wing, at Pasni, between Jask and Karachi.

Sir Samuel Hoare's party with the DH66 on Imperial Airways' inaugural flight to India, January 1927. Sir Samuel Hoare is seventh from left, next to him is Lady Maud Hoare. Captain Woolley Dod, the pilot, is fourth from left.

THE ARABIAN ROUTE

Imperial Airways could only adopt the Arabian coast route if an overnight stopping place could be established in the lower Gulf. This was as crucial to the southern route as Rutbah Wells had been to the Alexandria-Baghdad stage of the journey. It would involve Europeans living in a region where they had never lived before. This understandably caused concern to the sheikhs and their people in the Trucial States, the area targeted by Imperial Airways. In spring of 1932 the deadline on the Persian agreement had run out and Imperial Airways were into temporary extensions of a few months at a time. No agreement had been reached with Ras al Khaimah or Dubai, Abu Dhabi was too far away, and the east coast, which they would have preferred because it was nearer to Gwadar, had too difficult a coastline.

At this point, Sheikh Sultan bin Saqr of Sharjah wrote to the British offering facilities in his emirate. The British Political Resident, Sir Hugh Biscoe, went promptly to Sharjah to sign the agreement but by then Sheikh Sultan had met with opposition from his relatives and postponed the deal. Negotiations dragged on until July, when Sir Hugh asked Colonel Harold Dickson (political agent in Kuwait) to accompany him. Dickson spoke excellent Arabic, knew the Gulf well, and spent much of his time with Arab friends.

The weather was very hot; Sir Hugh was under great pressure from the British government to conclude the agreement quickly; tension was high. Perhaps the stress was too great, for on board ship en route to Sharjah, Sir

The giant HP42 biplanes had names of legendary heroes. Here 'Helena' stands at Croydon.

The luxurious interior of a HP42.

their food; a typical lunch out of Gwadar, for instance, consisted of lobster mayonnaise, chicken, ham and salad, pears, and cream cheese and biscuits. The Captain would join the passengers and socialise over the meal.

Smoking was not allowed in the air, because of the fire risk in a still partly fabric covered plane. The interior was reasonably quiet, however, as Agatha Christie described in *Death in the Clouds*: "The noise of the engine was skillfully deadened. There was no need to put cottonwool in the ears. Nevertheless there was enough noise to discourage conversation and encourage thought." Passengers enjoyed a reasonable baggage allowance, especially if they themselves were thin. The passenger and his luggage were weighed together, the total weight allowed being 200 lb.

The Hannibals flew a twice-weekly schedule out to India until the summer of 1940. They must have been some of the safest airliners ever. In 10 years of service they had flown 10 million miles with no injury at all to any of their passengers. Indeed, by 1933 insurance rates for Imperial Airways passengers were slightly better than those for boat or train journeys. The Hannibals were handed over to the RAF early in the war, and then the original Hannibal was lost in 1940 over the sea between Sharjah and Jask.

The Arabian coast

The route along the Arabian shores of the Gulf was opened in October 1932, and followed the trail laid out by the RAF in their pioneering surveys. Imperial Airways passengers would spend the night at the Shaibah airport near Basra, leave there in the early morning for Kuwait (an optional stop) then on to Bahrain where they had lunch. From Bahrain the route lay over Doha, Sirr Bani Yas island, Abu Dhabi and so to Sharjah, where they arrived in the evening.

A HP42 refuelling at Sharjah in 1937, en route for Basra.

For Imperial's first few flights along the Gulf, the RAF continued their protective role. On October 5, one of 203 Squadron's Rangoons was stationed on Sirr Bani Yas, to lend a hand in case of trouble. They waited to see the westbound flight through, the following day, and were back again the next week to keep a watchful eye on both eastward and westward bound flights.

The *Imperial Airways Gazette* described the new route thus: "The Imperial Airways machines will probably fly just off the coast for most of the way, and this will add to the attractions of the journey. Unadulterated desert, we believe, gets wearisome to the air traveller after a few hours, but water always looks charming from the air, especially when there are plenty of islands." They were right. A VIP passenger, the Secretary of State for Air, wrote enthusiastically of the flight: "It was a wonderful day and the flight to Shargah over the Gulf was indescribably beautiful." And the water from low altitude was indeed appealing, as another passenger, writing in the *Sydney Morning Herald* confirmed: "We flew low over the Gulf, and at 300 feet could clearly see hundreds of sharks, stingrays, sea snakes, and a few tortoises."

The ports of call each had their own interest, making this a particularly picturesque part of the journey. In Kuwait the airstrip was just outside the city walls. Passengers described these as great mud walls, seven miles long with watchtowers and loopholes. Camels and donkeys came and went through the gateway, on top of which fluttered the windstocking.

The *Imperial Gazette* promised passengers an agreeable lunch break in Bahrain: "Bahrein is the centre of a large pearl fishery. The capital is Manameh and there is an aerodrome there . . .. The stop at Manameh for lunch is sure to be an interesting break in the journey, for it is a pleasant place, possessed of many vineyards and natural wells which yield water of a temperature of 84 degrees all the year round." For passengers on the first flight out, it was perhaps more interesting than they bargained for. After lunch, as their plane taxied out, it sank into a forgotten water channel and could not be pulled out. The passengers spent the night in Manama, accommodated in private houses, until finally they could take off again next day.

The flight along the Gulf came to a close with the ascent to 7,500 feet, to clear the Hajar mountains between Sharjah and Dibba. They were a barrier which had caused some concern to Imperial Airways, prompting an urgent search for an emergency landing ground on the eastern side, in case planes failed to clear them on their way to or from Sharjah on the west side.

HP42 'Hanno' being pulled out of the sand in Bahrain.

Kuwait from the air in 1935, with fish traps in the foreground.

Emergency airstrips

Frequent emergency landing grounds were important to any pilot in those days, and for a commercial airline they were essential. Apart from the risk of engine trouble, airline pilots ran their planes on a minimum fuel calculation, since more fuel meant less load, and pilots were left a free hand when refuelling. Fortunately the RAF had already been at work along the Arabian coast before Imperial Airways flights started. Between Kuwait and Bahrain they had established two airstrips, on Jinna and Tarut islands, since King Abd al Aziz preferred them to keep to the islands.

South of Bahrain, a good flat area near Doha had been recorded but permission to use it not granted, as was the case with Abu Dhabi. The RAF had, however, marked out a landing ground and installed a fuel tank on the island of Sirr Bani Yas (which seemed to them sufficiently remote to need no permit). Sheikh Shakhbut of Abu Dhabi disagreed, and asked them to remove their fuel tank. He wrote to the British Political Agent (his protest arousing the great indignation of the British representative) that his island had been ruined by the airstrip there, an argument invariably used today each time a new airport is proposed for England. However, the airline really needed emergency airstrips on Bani Yas and at Abu Dhabi. Sheikh Shakhbut eventually agreed to them in 1934, in exchange for Britain sending geologists to search for water on Abu Dhabi island, and 5,000 rupees in lieu of rent.

The east coast of the peninsula was an even more vital area in which to have a landing strip, and even more difficult to negotiate. The RAF had already established airstrips at Sohar and Muscat, but another, more northerly one was essential, given the long sea crossing and the height of the mountains there. It was decided that Kalba would be the best site. Sheikh Saeed bin Hamad of Kalba was agreeable to the project, provided that Kalba (which was part of Sharjah territory) should be recognised as an independent emirate by the British. The deal was concluded. Imperial Airways got its emergency airstrip and fuel store; Kalba became independent in 1936 (regardless of the promise made four years earlier to Sheikh Sultan of Sharjah), and remained so until 1951 when it

The Hajar mountains were a formidable barrier for early planes.

A HP42 at Kuwait, 1934.

was reabsorbed into Sharjah territory again.

In fact the emergency airstrips were rarely needed by the airliners, although their presence must have been a great comfort. Occasionally an airliner did have to come down in the desert, but then it was on open sand. One pilot recalled having to land his Hannibal on a saltflat near Jubail in a storm. It landed safely but stuck in the mud. Local Arabs came across to the plane, then brought out a tent and organised a feast for the passengers and crew; in the morning they pulled the plane out of the mud with their donkeys. Imperial Airways sent an inscribed gold watch to their headman, in thanks.

One summer evening in August 1936, a plane left Basra for Bahrain late at night. Unfortunately the messages announcing its coming were not received in Bahrain, so no lights were on at the airport and the plane overflew the island in the dark. It continued southwards, looking for the airport lights, until 100 miles later it ran out of fuel, but managed to land safely in the desert where it was found by search planes the next day.

Already by 1934 another hazard had been foreseen, and that was the danger of collision in the air. By then, so many planes were flying along the empire routes that regulation was needed. So pilots were directed to fly along specific air corridors, and to keep to the right if they saw another aircraft approaching.

A local service

In the early days, planes became almost more familiar than cars in the towns of the Gulf. Local people there soon took eagerly to flying, as well as to using the regular air mail service now available on their doorstep. The flights were particularly welcome to pearl merchants who could send their pearls, a commodity of low weight and high value, on to India in a matter of one or two days, when it would have taken a week by boat. The pearl merchants used the planes widely to travel up and down the Gulf themselves, and general merchants began to import fresh food by plane, especially fresh fruit from Karachi to Bahrain.

Several Gulf sheikhs became fond of flying and made extensive journeys by air. Probably the first Gulf residents to take a trip by air were Sheikh Abdullah bin Isa and Sheikh Mohammad bin Abdullah of Bahrain, who went up for a flight during a visit to Britain in 1919. The airline linked the Gulf states with the outside world more immediately and more firmly than shipping could ever do.

Ever eastwards

Once the route to Karachi was in action, Imperial Airways began straight away to negotiate the more ambitious route right through to Australia. The total distance covered, 13,000 miles, would be by far the longest air route in the world. In 1933 Imperial linked up with Qantas, the Australian airline, to put in a joint bid for the route, and were successful.

Imperial Airways ordered a new plane for the Australia route, a four-engined de Havilland biplane airliner of the DH86 Diana class. This airliner was capable of a top speed of 170 mph, it could fly at a height of four miles, but carried only 10 passengers in its large and luxurious saloon.

The early 1930s was a period of rapid expansion for the airline. In 1932 they established their route along the Arabian shore of the Gulf, and also opened an air mail service to South Africa (passenger services having begun in 1931). In 1933 they began to fly as far east as Singapore, and in 1934 their empire network was completed with the first flight through to Darwin on the north coast of Australia. This longest of journeys took 12½ days to complete and the cost of a ticket was £180.

Imperial's passengers made 35 stops at airstrips along the route from England to Australia. Now, six decades later, when passengers might make only one stop on the way, it is remarkable to find that almost all the old Imperial airstrips have survived as airports in their own right. Only two, those of Gaza and Rutbah Wells, have disappeared from the map. The 1930s were the great days of Imperial Airways, with their huge biplanes forging their way across the world. World War II, which began late in 1939, severely affected civil aviation. In the following year, 1940, Imperial Airways became the British Overseas Airways Corporation (BOAC), and the last of the venerable Handley Page Hannibal biplanes flew home through the Gulf.

It was not the end of the route to the east, however, although there were some interruptions

The sun-helmeted crew of a HP42 during a refuelling stop at Gwadar. 'Hannibal', the first of the HP42s, was finally lost between Jask, along the coast from Gwadar, and Sharjah in 1940.

along the way. Most of the passengers were now in uniform (a traveller in civilian clothes remarked that he felt quite out of place), the cabins were more spartan, and there were no attentive stewards. Sleek monoplanes had at last replaced the towering wings of the biplanes.

In 1940, also, most of the Mediterranean shores and islands were taken by the Germans and the crossing became too dangerous for British aircraft. The direct route from Britain to the east was closed. However, BOAC continued to run a 'horseshoe route' from South Africa to Cairo, and then on along the Gulf, via India to Australia as before.

When the war ended, commercial aviation really took off. Soon there were 20 services a week flying through Bahrain, by then the busiest airport in the Gulf, since fewer stopping places were needed along the route. Sharjah airport was busy also, with four or five flights a day being recorded, but most of them were RAF planes.

Jet engines, developed during the war, were introduced into airliners in the 1950s; the great Boeing 707, first of a distinguished line of successful jet airliners, took to the air in 1954. In the 1960s air travel became the major means of mass transport, overtaking ships and trains for long journeys. BOAC, which was already flying to

Bahrain and Sharjah, started a regular service to Dubai in 1967, then to Abu Dhabi, and soon after to Muscat and Doha.

Supersonic flight came to the Gulf in 1976, with the start of a Concorde service to Bahrain. An inaugural VIP lunch of smoked salmon, roast duckling, strawberries and cream was served on the opening flight, made at faster than the speed of sound. Concorde flew at 1,350 mph, and made the journey in less than four hours, but the rise in oil prices in the mid-1970s made the service uneconomic and it was discontinued by the end of the decade.

Today the airline has changed its name again, and BOAC has become British Airways. Her modern airliners, and those of many other nations as well, stream through the Gulf where all the airports are busier than ever before. Today's planes cruise at 500 mph, fly at 35,000 feet and carry up to 350 passengers per flight. Some are capable of flying from the Far East to Europe direct, but for most flights a stopping place half way is still welcome. And that stopping place is usually one of the airports on the Arabian shore of the Gulf. The old Imperial Airways route laid down sound foundations for the needs of civil aviation of the future.

Concorde flew London-Bahrain in less than four hours, in the 1970s.

Les Vowles
93

FLYING BOATS

In the mid-1930s Imperial Airways saw an opportunity for a profitable expansion of their operations to the Far East. Although the airline had received a government subsidy in the early days, the goal set for them had always been one of self-sufficiency – a commercial operation. In 1934 the airline suggested a government contract for them to carry air mail as far as Sydney at ordinary British postage stamp rates. The quantity of mail to be carried was estimated at 2,000 tons a year and the contract would be worth £750,000 per annum.

Once the contract was agreed, Imperial Airways ordered 28 giant flying boats, at a cost of £1.5 million, to run the new air mail service. The airline had always liked the idea of using flying boats on the route to the east. They would be safer over open water – a flying boat obliged to make a forced landing on the sea might stay afloat and taxi into harbour, whereas a land plane would certainly sink, and they could land easily on any stretch of sheltered water. From the very beginning of their service to the east, the airline had used flying boats to cross the Mediterranean, Calcutta flying boats built by Short Brothers.

The early surveys carried out for them had also been made by flying boats. The first survey flight for a commercial route to Australia was made in 1926 by Sir Alan Cobham, flying in a de Havilland 50 adapted as a seaplane. His journey was not altogether plain sailing: over the marshes of Iraq his mechanic was killed by a stray bullet fired from the ground, which unfortunately hit the plane. A day or two later, when he tried to take off from Bushire on the Persian coast in six to eight foot waves, he collided with the Consul's launch.

Short's S23 Empire flying boats carried mail and passengers via the Gulf to the Far East.

Passengers prepare to board Cameronian *on the Nile.*
The river steamer Mayflower *was used as a passenger resthouse.*

One of the earliest pictures of Dubai's creek, taken in 1932 by an Imperial Airways steward.

where they taxied in, there is no water at all; land has been reclaimed and the shore is far away.

The major problem for Imperial Airways was the stopping place on the UAE coast. Sharjah creek was not suitable for flying boats, so Imperial surveyed Umm al Quwain and Dubai creeks. They decided that Dubai was the better creek and in July signed an agreement with Sheikh Saeed for the use of the creek for one year. They would have the use of a 1,800-yard reach of the creek near where the Maktoum bridge now stands, and the right to install refuelling facilities.

The rent was a modest 440 rupees a month. The following year, when the agreement was renewed, Sheikh Saeed realised that his creek could be worth more than that. He demanded, and obtained, 940 rupees a month for use of the creek, 500 rupees a month personal subsidy, and five rupees landing fees (very similar to the charges for Sharjah airport).

Dubai was in fact a most convenient choice for Imperial Airways, since flying boat passengers could be driven across to the resthouse at Sharjah for meals or to spend the night. The route between the two had already been inspected by an English officer before the Sharjah airport

opened. He concluded: "The road to Dibai is quite practicable for wheeled transport and only has loose sand in two places. At these places all passengers have to get out and push. The journey takes ³/₄ of an hour".

The Empire flying boats came into use on the Gulf route at the beginning of October 1937, just five years after the Hannibals had first flown here. They ran a twice or three times weekly service, soon extending as far as Australia, and this continued throughout the war, increasing to four times a week by the end of the war.

The air mail service proved more of a success than Imperial had bargained for. Christmas mail was always the high spot of the year. In 1936 their land planes had carried 27 tons of Christmas mail; the following year the seaplanes carried 81 tons. In December 1938, however, just a year after the Empires' mail service had started, Imperial were completely overwhelmed by an avalanche of Christmas mail to the east. They just managed to carry the 222 tons of mail dispatched from England, but only by chartering planes wherever they could find them. This mail crisis was not to be repeated, however, for by the following Christmas Europe was at war.

Test letter sent from Sydney to London by Empire flying boat in 1938. It took 11 days.

After the fall of France, Empire flying boats pioneered a route looping across Africa, running from Southampton via Lisbon, Lagos, Khartoum or Cairo, to join up with the service from South Africa. From there they were able to continue northwards on their traditional route to Baghdad and thence via the Gulf to the Far East. The South Africa/Far East route became known as the 'horseshoe', and most of the passengers carried along it were in military uniform.

Flying boats continued to use the Gulf route for a few more years after the end of the war. By then they were Short Sunderlands which stopped at Kuwait, Bahrain and Dubai, but their days were coming to an end. Civil flying boats ceased to operate along the route altogether in 1949. In Bahrain their moorings, jetty and Marine Airport were handed over to the RAF; BP Aviation Service who shared the jetty must, they said, continue to have use of it.

The flying boat Scipio was a regular visitor to Dubai and Ras al Khaimah creeks during the early 1930s.

THE SEARCH
FOR OIL

Oil companies are to aeroplanes as the camel is to the bedouin, so close in fact that the one could not have existed without the other. And as, too, the bedu could hardly have survived without his camels, so the oil companies would have found prospecting extremely difficult without the help of planes. One oilman, speaking of the southern Gulf, concluded that the Iraq Petroleum Company simply could not have operated there without the support of Gulf Aviation (now Gulf Air), and Gulf Aviation could not have existed without the work provided by the oil company.

The dependency was, of course, even greater than that. Planes run on fuel derived from the crude oil extracted and refined by the companies. Without this fuel, the aeroplane engine could not have been developed; without a constant, vast and reliable supply of fuel, airports would grind to a halt. Even the little oil camp airstrips, which were to accompany the oilmen throughout the deserts of Arabia, were stocked with piles of fuel drums.

It was the oilmen who brought aeroplanes into the remotest deserts, introducing them to the hazards of landing among the sands in a way which even the old RAF furrow across the deserts of Syria and Iraq had never done. And for the geophysical parties surveying areas of desert known only to the sparsely scattered bedouin, the small planes which brought their food and supplies were a lifeline, their most vital link with the outside world.

From their earliest days in Arabia, oilmen realised that in the desert an aeroplane must be the answer. When American geologists first landed

Visit of the Wali of Ibri, Oman, Sayed Sa'oud bin Harib, to the 'spudding-in' of the Yibal 1 oil well.

47

on the shores of Saudi Arabia's eastern province in 1933, they hired camels and set off across the sands to look for the geological structures which just might indicate the presence of oil deep below the ground. Camels are, of course, an excellent way of travelling across the sands. But no one could claim they are rapid, and in the eastern province the sands are vast.

The following year the geologists obtained permission to bring in a small plane, and were supplied with a Fairchild, which scoured the region taking photographs of signs of likely rock folding. The surveying parties directed the plane from the ground by digging an arrow-shaped depression in the sand, sprinkling it with gasoline and firing it, leaving thus a clear black arrow to point the way. After five years of thankless toil, they finally discovered oil in the Damam Dome, and made their first shipment in summer of 1939, just before World War II was to interrupt their operations. When the oil company Aramco resumed work after the war, its teams were constantly supported by aircraft, and a major airbase had been constructed by the US government in Dhahran.

IPC explores

The oil industry in the lower Gulf owes its existence to the pioneering efforts of the Iraq Petroleum Company in the years just before and after World War II. IPC was itself a large, international company whose partners in the post-war period were Anglo-Iranian (now British Petroleum), Shell, the French Compagnie Française des Pétroles, the American Socony-Vacuum and New Jersey companies, and Calouste Gulbenkian with his famous five percent share. It had evolved from an earlier consortium in 1929 to develop the oil industry in Iraq, but by the 1930s, after the discovery of oil in Bahrain, IPC realised that there was a distinct possibility of finding oil elsewhere in the Gulf.

The Iraq Petroleum Company had early come to appreciate the advantages of air travel, and from the beginning of 1933 used planes chartered from Imperial Airways to transport their personnel. The Avro 10 and de Havilland DH 50 were the first used, followed by the de Havilland Dragon, forerunner of the Rapide. Each of the 12 main pumping stations along the pipeline to the

An IPC DH84 Dragon, circa 1934.

A Yibal 1 'Christmas tree'.

A Blackburn Beverley heavy transport plane at Baghdad airport, 1955.

Mediterranean had its own landing ground; one kindly station superintendent endeared himself to the pilots by popping planes' sparking plugs into the oven along with their breakfasts before dawn on a cold morning, to ensure a smooth start up. For the pipeline's official opening ceremony, in January 1935, at which King Ghazi of Iraq officiated, the company leased an airliner from Imperial Airways, and a fleet of smaller planes, to transport guests along the pipeline to ceremonies at either end.

In the following years, IPC obtained oil concessions elsewhere along the Gulf, in Qatar, the Trucial States and Oman; one of the partners, Anglo-Persian, had already obtained a share in the concession for Kuwait. IPC set up operating companies for the individual countries: Petroleum Development (Qatar), Petroleum Development (Trucial Coast), Petroleum Development (Oman).

Their contracts were all onshore. After the war, however, offshore concessions also became available and two of the partners, Anglo-Iranian and Compagnie Francaise des Petroles, obtained the offshore concessions for Abu Dhabi and Dubai in 1952.

Desert airstrips

Prospecting throughout the Gulf started in the years immediately before World War II, with successful results in both Kuwait and Qatar where oil was struck just before the war, but could not be exploited until after the war. In the Trucial States and Oman, however, survey parties had only just started their work. They were not able to resume activities until the late 1940s. Then geophysical teams were sent out to explore far and wide.

They bumped over the desert in trucks equipped with wide tyres, or Land Rovers if they were lucky, and set up camp among the dunes or on coastal sabkhas, wherever further seismic studies seemed worthwhile, or trial wells might be dug. One of the first considerations in choosing a camp site, if it was to be at all long-lasting, was the need for an airstrip. A flat area of ground would be cleared, marked out with oil drums, equipped with a windstocking, an aircraft radio beacon and a radio set, and they were in business. If planes came in at night, the landing ground could be easily lit with paraffin flares. Years later these old desert camp sites could still be recognised by the litter of oil drums and the skeleton of a windstocking.

"We asked them to find a strip about 1,200 yards long, or better still 1,500 yards if they could manage it. We could put anything down on a strip like that," remarked Dennis Hanbury, who was IPC's Aviation Superintendent in the 1950s and 1960s. He was himself by then a veteran pilot, having flown the Imperial Airways HP42s along the Gulf in the mid-1930s, and fought as an RAF pilot during the war.

Hanbury had to find sufficient planes to service all the oil camps out in the desert. They needed equipment, supplies, fresh food, mail, and the ability to join, or leave, their remote camp. IPC owned about nine de Havilland Doves which were kept at an airfield at Tripoli in Lebanon, and maintained there by Airwork who also provided the crews. They were much in demand for IPC work in Iraq as well. A plane would be sent down the Gulf from Tripoli for a couple of days at a time, but this was never enough to cover all the camps in the region. After a while the Doves began to stay longer, flying out to Qatar, on to Tarif in Abu Dhabi, and finally down to Muscat, before returning to Tripoli. Eventually Hanbury obtained a Dove full time, for this area alone. It was based in Bahrain and maintained by Gulf Aviation, but the pilots worked directly for IPC. Then it became possible to run a regular daily service to Tarif, Sharjah, Fahud and other drilling sites, as well as to the geophysical parties in the field. The support base for most of these services was Dukhan in Qatar.

Douglas DC3 Dakotas were the 'workhorses' of airline and oil company travel and transport.

A Blackburn Beverley transport plane – large enough to have carried an entire oil rig from Qatar to Fahud in one trip.

A wounded man being helped from the palm-frond terminal building of Ibri airport to a plane, for transfer to Muscat hospital.

The service was literally a lifeline to the men out in the camps. In the case of accident or illness, their position would have been desperate without the planes. On one occasion, one of the small helicopters, based at Tarif for seismic surveys, crashed. The injured pilot was quickly flown out by plane to hospital in Bahrain and saved; on another occasion, a worker injured by a jet of gas was also evacuated in time.

When the two IPC partners, Anglo-Iranian and Compagnie Française des Petroles, obtained the offshore concession for Abu Dhabi in 1952, Hanbury advised the Anglo-Iranian prospecting party that their first priority should be the development of a really good landing ground on Das Island. They followed his advice and were to thank him for it later. Planes to Das Island were their major supply line just as, once production started, helicopters would provide the supply line across the sea to the rigs themselves.

Airstrips had been the priority, too, in Oman where Edward Henderson set up the Petroleum Development base camp at Duqm, as he relates in *This Strange Eventful History*. To start with, they sent a plane along the coast to take aerial photographs of possible beaches where they could land supplies and establish an airstrip. From the photos they chose Duqm, on a virtually uninhabited stretch of coast of the Jiddat al Harasis. They shipped in a huge load of petrol in metal jerrycans and set out a landing ground adequate for the company's small Doves. Their first airstrip was too close to the sea and became sodden at high tides, but a second strip, a little further from the shore, was satisfactory. Duqm would supply the drilling camp at Fahud, deep in the interior.

Perhaps the most challenging freight problem that the oil company faced during those years was the delivery of their first oil rig to Fahud. Deep in the desert, way behind the mountain barrier, Fahud was remote from any permanent habitation or motorable tracks, totally inaccessible for anything like an oil rig. In this case they borrowed a Blackburn Beverley heavy transport plane from the RAF, and set their engineers the task of packing the rig, its diesels and pumps all into the one aircraft. They succeeded and the rig was successfully flown from Qatar to Fahud. However, the well was dry and in 1960, after other failed attempts, three of the IPC partners withdrew from

Petroleum Development (Oman) leaving only Shell and a minority shareholding to Gulbenkian. The persistence of the remaining partners was rewarded: in 1964 they finally struck oil at Fahud, only 400 yards away from the original dry well!

The planes

De Havilland Doves, first flown in 1945, were the key planes operated by the oilmen during the great prospecting decade of the 1950s. They were sturdy planes which would go anywhere and despite all the rough trips and rougher landings that they made, not one was lost in the Gulf at that time. The Dove could carry light equipment and up to eight passengers, and cruised at around 140 mph. IPC owned its own Doves and also chartered more from Gulf Aviation, whose founder's eagerness to own this versatile plane sadly cost him his life, as will be discussed in the Gulf Airlines chapter.

The versatile de Havilland Dove.

They also chartered Gulf Aviation's original planes, the small ex-World War II fabric-bodied Avro Ansons, and later on their Douglas DC3 Dakotas. The Dakota had first flown some 20 years earlier, in 1936, and was to continue in use for forty years more. It was the most successful transport plane ever built, the main workhorse of civil aviation in the decades following the war, just as it had been for the military who used more than 12,000 of them during the war.

For heavier loads the company chartered Vickers Vikings, planes closely based on the wartime Wellington bomber, from Airwork who ran a weekly service bringing staff out from England to Dukhan in Qatar. These planes could carry up to 36 passengers; they also delivered food and equipment to the camps. Another freight plane used for deliveries of this kind was the Avro York, its design based this time on the wartime Lancaster

bomber; it was chartered from Trans Mediterranean Airlines. These planes were used especially for the delivery of fresh fruit and vegetables from Lebanon to the Oman main camp at Azaiba, which superseded Duqm once Fahud was set up. One oilman remembers flying into Azaiba on such a delivery run when, just as the pilot came in to land, a line of donkeys trotted out across the dirt runway. It was too late to pull up into the air again, disaster seemed imminent. But just at that moment a gap in the donkey line appeared; the pilot slewed his plane towards the gap, his passenger held his breath, and miraculously they squeezed through, missing the donkeys by a hair's breadth.

Throughout the Gulf, the oil companies cleared landing grounds in the most unlikely looking corners of the bleakest desert. It was, after all, not what was on the ground but what was beneath it that interested them. In Iraq and Kuwait they had had some 50 years of airstrip building by the time the Gulf War broke out. Commanders of the coalition forces in that war were delighted to find, from aerial reconnaissance, that when they advanced into Kuwait they had a choice of hundreds of dirt airstrips on which to land supplies. Logistics were made that much easier for them by these old oil company airstrips.

Sheikh Shakhbut descends from a Middle East Airlines plane at the old Abu Dhabi airport.

AIRSTRIPS TO AIRPORTS

The low-lying desert surface along the Arabian shores of the Gulf rises almost imperceptibly from the sea; close to the shore, it consists often of sabkha – or salt flats. When dry, which is most of the year, these salt flats are smooth and hard, perfectly suitable for landing a plane.

Much of the rest of the desert is firm and reasonably flat also; it is not too difficult a job to clear a dirt runway. Indeed, so simple a task did it seem to the pioneers of aviation in the Gulf that 203 Squadron reported on the airstrip that they established in 1932 at Sohar: "The small amount of work entailed in turning a bare stretch of land into a serviceable landing ground was undertaken by him (the Wali of Sohar) personally."

The early RAF flyers cleared dozens of landing grounds of this type along both shores of the Gulf. Today some of those runways are still just visible to the eye at ground level, and much clearer from above. Many of the emergency landing grounds on the Imperial Airways route are now forgotten; some of them have disappeared completely under the buildings of rapidly expanding towns.

All the airstrips on the Arabian shore cleared for Imperial Airways' main stopping places, however, have developed into large international airports, even if several of them have moved a few miles down the road. Today they are equipped with the most up-to-date radar, radio communications and instrument landing systems, and accommodate the world's largest and most modern aircraft on a daily basis. Where once a single light, such as the beacon on the Sharjah fort, guided planes in to land, now vast runways lit by 3,000 airport lights make the night as bright as day. The simple sheds

The old wind tower building which was Abu Dhabi's original airport.

A windstocking floated over one of Kuwait's city gates in the 1930s, to guide planes which landed beside the walls.

which once served as passenger shelters have been replaced by magnificent terminal buildings, making this one of the most interesting regions for airport architecture in the world.

Kuwait

Kuwait was the first stopping place on the Arabian coast route. It was originally an optional halt, the plane putting down only if a passenger requested to get off there; it was so close to the main station at Basra that there was no great need for refuelling. Gradually it was used more and more, however, and planes took the opportunity to refuel there too.

Passengers found this landing ground, close beside Kuwait's long mud city wall which had recently been repaired during the raids of the Ikhwan bedouin, one of the most picturesque on the journey and there are many descriptions of it. A military report on the route just before it opened commented: "Kuwait aerodrome is reported good though on the small side, being about 600 yards square. It is close to the city wall on the south east side. The approaches are good except for the wall. This however provides excellent shelter from the shemal as aircraft are able to taxi right up to it."

Violet Dickson (wife of Col. Harold Dickson) recalled in her memoirs that originally this airfield

had no amenities other than a wind sock and a stack of petrol cans for refuelling. The townspeople soon became used to the arrival of the great biplanes, and cars and bicycles rushed out across the sand to meet them. This was the closest of all the Gulf airports to the homes of the people.

Violet Dickson recalled a great storm in 1934 which, despite the shelter of the wall, ripped the fabric covering the wing of the plane. Its passengers had to be collected by another of the Hannibals, while the plane waited there. Eventually the necessary materials were brought to Kuwait and the wing repaired, only to be struck that night by another storm which again ripped the wing. The plane finally left Kuwait two months behind schedule.

She also recalled another, more serious mishap during the war, when an RAF plane missed Kuwait in a storm and crashed into the sea near Failaka island. Her husband was urged that he must find this plane at all costs, it carried 'very important documents'. Days of searching were to no avail. It was only months later that they learnt that the 'documents' were actually the Iraqi crown jewels, and thousands of dinars in cash.

A few years later, Kuwait airport might have saved a KLM Douglas C54, which was unable to land in Basra in 1953 because of bad visibility. The pilot decided to fly on to Dhahran, but ran out of petrol and crash landed in the desert 17 miles short of the airport. His 56 passengers and 10 crew were all saved, but the pilot was reprimanded for not having thought of Kuwait, instead of trying to reach Dhahran.

After the war, Kuwait's airstrip was used largely by the Kuwait Oil Company, bringing fresh fruit and vegetables in from the Lebanon and flying their workers to India in Douglas DC3s. They had a radio in a tent beside the runway, serving as their control tower. During the late 1940s ordinary passengers travelled by the BOAC flying boat service which came into Kuwait twice weekly.

As Kuwait city expanded, the walls were knocked down to give way to roads and buildings. In February 1962 the Kuwait International Airport was established on a flat desert plain, ten miles south of the original city. Today the suburbs of the town extend virtually to the edge of the airport.

A new and ultra-modern terminal, designed by the Japanese architect Kenzo Tange and built by Dutch contractors, was completed in 1979 to replace the original terminal. This new terminal building is in the shape of a giant aircraft, which it resembles closely when seen from above. The wings serve as the arrival and departure areas, while the long body of the building leads to the

The ultra-modern control tower of Kuwait's airport today.

arrival and departure gates. Access to the planes is via 13 telescopic bridges extending out from the terminal. In the 1980s the old terminal building, to the west of the new one, was upgraded to provide additional space.

After the liberation of Kuwait in February 1991, the airport went through a tremendous process of rebuilding. Today Kuwait airport has surpassed the state of development which it reached prior to the Iraqi invasion and by mid-1995 it was serving 35 international scheduled airlines.

Bahrain

The original airstrip on Bahrain was near to Manama, close to the Gudaibiya palace. It was considered in the military report to be a "very poor" landing ground, especially in a shemal. The RAF had already looked at a stretch of desert on Muharraq island which they considered much better, but there was no causeway at the time (it opened only in 1940), and ferrying the passengers by dhow seemed a daunting prospect.

The officer inspecting the route did, however, go across to Muharraq where he found a quite flat and very hard plain, some 2,000 by 1,100 yards in extent. He motored over it at 35 mph without feeling a bump. He was impressed and thought that if the flooding said to cover it at high tide were not too bad, this might be a better option. It might even, he thought, be worth the expense of putting in a telephone line!

The *Imperial Airways Gazette* account of the route just before it opened remarked that the aerodrome was at Manama, but "a second aerodrome has been constructed on the island of Muharraq". Evidently they were not sure of their ground in Manama, but the "constructed" sounds optimistic for the Muharraq plain. Nevertheless it must have been clear enough to see, for when the pilot of the first flight to Bahrain, which stuck in a silted water channel in taking off, did finally get his plane into the air, he flew straight across to Muharraq and landed there. From then on, Imperial Airways used the Muharraq ground.

Over the next five years several passengers gave descriptions of the Muharraq landing ground, published in Imperial's Gazette. A year after the route opened a passenger noted that it was "on a stretch of sandy soil with no signs of substantial buildings within sight." The following year a passenger remarked that there was "a small woven grass shelter to keep out the stinging and

The original palm-frond terminal building at Bahrain's old airport.

rather cold wind." Beside this barasti shelter was a signpost pointing to London in one direction and Karachi in the other. There too was a big brass bell which announced the movement of planes: four bells for an approaching plane, six bells ready for take off.

Five years after the opening of the airstrip, a few temporary structures were appearing; an aide of the Maharajah of Baroda, who was travelling on Imperial Airways, recorded that "the aerodrome buildings consisted of tents and huts in a vast sandy waste." This 'waste' however did provide an excellent landing ground, rated at the time "the finest natural aerodrome between England and India."

During World War II, and up to 1971 when the British left the Gulf (and of course again during the Gulf War in the winter of 1990-91), Muharraq airport was used as an extremely active RAF aerodrome as well as an increasingly busy civil airport. By 1940 there were permanent terminal buildings there, and a new control tower with an air raid siren was built. Mechanics still had to carry their tools in buckets of cold water, however, for

there was no air-conditioning there in the early years of the war, though by 1943 the air-conditioning plants were installed and staff were urged to make good use of them.

In the 1960s the runways were extended by means of land infill along the shores of Muharraq island. A handsome new terminal building was opened in 1961; it was known for a large mural in the transit lounge showing Bahrain's long history. By the mid-1960s some 1,200 civil flights a month were recorded at the airport which had, among other services, become the main supply centre for oil company personnel working throughout the southern Gulf.

In the 1980s the first phase of a major upgrading of Muharraq airport terminal was completed, providing greatly expanded facilities. By the end of the decade the airport was handling over 3.5 million passengers a year, and a second phase of improvement of the terminal was undertaken in the early 1990s. By that time, the airport's 12,500-foot runway could cater for any of the world's airliners.

Today's modern airport at Muharraq, Bahrain.

Sharjah

Sharjah was, as recounted in previous chapters, the lynchpin of Imperial Airways' route along the Arabian shore of the Gulf. It was here that passengers would stay the night, here that planes would come in to refuel from the longest leg of the journey across the sea and the Hajar mountains from Gwadar, here that the major staging post would be established. The landing ground chosen by the RAF needed to be a good one, and indeed it was excellent.

The stretch of flat sand, one and a half miles to the south-east of the town on the creek, was hard and level, with four inches of soft sand to ease the landing. "The surface is a peculiar brown colour" the inspector reported, "all the dark part is good to land on, but the light sand is softer." There was an area 1,000 by 800 yards of the dark sand, plenty of space for planes of those days, and so good was it that the only work needed was to mark out the landing area.

The proximity of the creek meant that building materials, fuel and supplies could easily be brought in by sea. A resthouse-cum-fort was built there in just a couple of months over the summer of 1932, and the first passengers landed there in October of that year. This was a brand new landing ground. Many others in the Gulf had been quietly used by the RAF for several years, but Sharjah airstrip was only marked out in May of that year. The first trial flight by an HP42 was made in June, and the first scheduled flight at the beginning of October.

Passengers enthused over the romantic and well-equipped resthouse, where they were served an excellent meal, enjoyed a hot bath and slept in comfortable beds. The little aerodrome was equipped with a wireless, and a powerful beacon visible 80 miles away, to guide planes safely in to land at night.

During and after World War II, Sharjah aerodrome was also used as a busy RAF base, and

The old fort/resthouse and the early control tower of Sharjah's first airport survive among modern development.

One of the last photos of the British military complex and airstrip at Sharjah, taken in 1970. The airstrip is now King Abd al Aziz Street.

Sharjah's elegant modern airport with domed terminal buildings.

by the end of the war was frequently visited by US air force planes too. These planes were still coming in to land on the 'dark brown sand' of the dirt runways. By the 1950s, however, the faster jet aircraft, which were by then in use, eroded the sand runways badly. In the following decade the runway was paved. It has survived intact until today as King Abd al Aziz street, with the King Faisal mosque built within the turning circle for planes at the end of it.

Development of the aerodrome was rapid during the 1960s, with extensive building projects being undertaken. A new terminal building was completed in 1968 by the Emirate of Sharjah, and the fort-resthouse was given a second lease of life as the air traffic control centre. But the old airport was nearing the end of its existence. By 1971, when it was handed over to Sharjah Emirate, the town was advancing rapidly on this historic airport, the first to be created in the UAE, and would soon surround it completely.

Clearly for Sharjah, as for Kuwait, a new airport farther away from the town had become essential. In the mid-1970s a new Sharjah International Airport was constructed some 10 miles away to the north-east of the old town, out on the road to Dhaid. This airport came into operation in 1977, used mostly for freight at first, but also taking

some passenger aircraft. The airport has become increasingly busy in the intervening years and by the mid-1990s extensions to the terminal buildings were planned. Sharjah's airport is one of the most charming in the Gulf. Its terminal consists of a group of domed buildings set on a slight rise above grassy banks, and flanked by an elegant small mosque.

Dubai

Dubai had been one of the early choices for a landing ground on the coast of the UAE, and by 1932 the RAF had already been testing the ground there. The inspection report of June of that year commented that "there is an excellent landing ground at Dibai about one and a half miles east of the town and close to the creek." This airstrip was not developed, however, since negotiations with Sharjah came to a fruitful conclusion. Instead Dubai creek was used as an alighting area for flying boats, which for a decade ran a regular service through there several times a week, until 1947.

The old Sharjah airport was on the Dubai side of Sharjah town, and was therefore initially a disincentive to the development of an airport in Dubai. However, in 1959 Sheikh Rashid decided that Dubai must have its own aerodrome, and in 1960 an airstrip was opened on a level stretch of sabkha, some two and a half miles east of the town. It had initially a 6,000-foot dirt runway; but this was soon given a hard surface and by summer of 1965 the airport received its first jet airliner, a de Havilland Comet. The original old terminal building still stands today, near the entrance to the Cargo Village. When replaced by a new terminal, it continued in use initially as a cargo terminal and a helicopter port.

With the expansion of Dubai, a larger airport was needed. In 1971 a very elegant terminal building, designed by architects Page and Broughton, was constructed some distance to the east of the original one. This new terminal was described by Alexander Frater in *Beyond the Blue Horizon*, a book retracing the old Imperial Airways route to Australia, as "small and extravagantly pretty, built around rows of slender columns with their tops spreading like date palms." These facilities were doubled in extent when the new arrivals terminal, designed by Bechtel, was added in the late 1980s; this building has a slightly different but harmonious and equally elegant design.

Air traffic through Dubai airport had soared in the 1970s and 1980s, reflecting not only the very rapid development of Dubai city, but also the fact that the Emirates' coast is still an essential stopping place for large numbers of flights from Europe to the Far East. Already by the end of the 1960s traffic was doubling annually (up from 81,473 passengers in 1967, to 135,299 the following year, for example); this increase accelerated during the 1970s so that by 1980 the airport was receiving 2.8 million passengers a year and 35 airlines.

By the mid-1990s more than 60 airlines were using Dubai airport, by now the busiest in the Gulf, and handling around six million passengers a year. Her two 13,200-foot concrete runways take the largest jet airliners, directed by modern air traffic control, radio and radar systems. Smooth operation of the airport has been assured throughout by DNATA, and the Duty Free shopping centre has become an international attraction after winning numerous awards; many airlines have opted for this airport because of its convenience, efficiency and appeal.

Dubai's large international airport is attractively designed.

Abu Dhabi

Abu Dhabi was not used as a regular landing ground by Imperial Airways, because they considered it too far from Gwadar to be feasible for planes of those days. However, it was used as an emergency airstrip after 1934, and it had already been surveyed as such before the airline started operations. The inspector reported that south of the small town of Abu Dhabi there was a long flat stretch of desert which appeared good for landing.

This airstrip, a few miles from the town, was used by the RAF and inherited by the oilmen when they first came to Abu Dhabi in the 1950s. It continued to be used by them during the 1960s, for both onshore and offshore oil exploration. The oilmen improved the surface of their airstrip by levelling, scraping and rolling it, to give a good landing area so long as conditions were dry. They marked it out with old oil drums and checked the area for stray camels before any plane came in to land. Their old control tower was in a small wind tower building which survived near the Abu Dhabi

radio tower into the 1980s. Eventually the Bateen airport was developed, farther away from the town, extending into the eastern tip of the island and ending close to the Muqta bridge. Today this airport, now greatly modernised, has continued in use as a military air base.

It was extensively developed in 1970, however, as Abu Dhabi's international airport, and was provided with surfaced runways and an attractive terminal building. However, traffic was increasing rapidly, and Abu Dhabi town was gradually extending across the whole island; expansion of the old airport had become impossible. By the late 1970s it was clear that Abu Dhabi, like Sharjah, would need to resite her airport farther away from the town.

In January 1982 a new and far larger international airport was opened on the mainland, close to the road running north to Dubai. This airport was designed by the architects of the Charles de Gaulle airport near Paris, and it reflects the design of that airport. There is a curved terminal building and a circular satellite with eleven telescopic piers providing access to planes. It was designed to

Abu Dhabi's third and present airport is far removed from the earliest wind tower airport buildings.

Bait al Falaj, Muscat.

handle five million passengers a year, but by the mid-1990s further expansion to double that capacity was already planned. There is a 13,500-foot runway to accommodate the largest jet airliners, as well as the most up-to-date radar, air traffic control and lighting systems.

The airport and the land around it are beautifully landscaped with lawns and flowering shrubs, and the road from the airport to the town some 20 miles away is lined on both sides by dense shrubberies. It is a far cry from the arid strip of sabkha, marked out in the 1930s as the first landing ground at Abu Dhabi.

Muscat

Muscat, on the east coast of the Oman peninsula, was a more challenging area in which to establish an airstrip. Here the mountains rise straight from the sea; there is no coastal plain of the sort which offered such an easy option to aerodrome makers at Sohar. In Muscat the creation of an airstrip was a difficult job, and access to it would always present a challenge to pilots.

The airmen of 203 Squadron needed to find a site close to the town which would serve at least as an emergency landing ground. Imperial's great airliners would not normally come in to Muscat, which was too far to the south of their route to be really useful. But an airstrip was needed there, should an airliner be blown off course over the

sea, or simply lose its way. The RAF would use this airstrip from time to time as a staging post, and also needed facilities there.

The search for a landing strip was not easy, and eventually they decided on Bait al Falaj valley. Their account of it sounds more like an apology: "It was not an ideal landing ground, but no other flat land existed within easy range of Muscat, and as it was considered suitable for the limited use to which it would be put by aircraft of the Royal Air Force, it was cleared of obstructions and marked out as an aerodrome."

Bait al Falaj continued in occasional use by the RAF, up to and during World War II, after which it dropped out of use following a crash there of an RAF Dakota. It was not until 1948 that oilmen reopened the old airstrip. Edward Henderson described how he set about rehabilitating the airstrip. It took 50 men two days to clear it sufficiently for the first aircraft, an old de Havilland Rapide, to land there since the war.

Like their predecessors in the RAF, the oilmen also considered Bait al Falaj a less than ideal airport. The mountains hemmed the valley in closely on either side, and closed off the inland end of it. It was too dangerous for a plane to take off towards this inland barrier, which would be difficult to clear; regardless of wind direction, planes must take off towards the sea. And as Henderson remarked, "even going out towards the sea meant taking a twisting course immediately after take-off, down the valley with the rocks too close to the wing tips, but one got used to it." He adds, however, that even in a jet aircraft of a later decade "some passengers may have felt a certain concern". A Department of Information book on Oman, published in 1972, endorses his view: "To land in a modern aircraft over the sea, with the wingtips of the aircraft almost touching the Jabal, as most passengers thought, was an unforgettable experience." Many travellers who landed at Bait al Falaj in the past would put it more strongly than that.

However, with the advent of jet planes in the 1950s, the airstrip was tarmacked. It continued to serve the oil company, military planes (especially those of the Omani air force after 1959), and from the early 1950s the small passenger planes of Gulf Aviation.

However, the airport could not take anything larger than the planes flying into it at that time, and even those managed it at a pinch, and in daytime only. One of the priorities of the new regime of Sultan Qaboos (who came to power in 1970) was to create an international airport which would be readily accessible to the increasingly large and rapid airliners of the day.

As Oman's road network spread across the country, more distant areas came within easy reach of the capital. Some miles to the north west of Muscat, the Batinah plain cuts a level swathe between the sea and the mountains. There at Seeb, 20 miles away from Muscat, a new international airport was rapidly constructed on flat land beside the sea. The runway was completed in 1972 and planes began to use it immediately; it was long enough to take the most demanding airliners of the time, Concorde and Boeing 747s. Several international airlines began to fly into Seeb soon after it opened, and by the mid-1970s it was handling 170,000 passengers a year. The terminal buildings, designed by N.V. Naco, Netherlands Airport Consultants and built by the Cyprus contractors Joannou and Paraskavides (J & P) were not completed until the following year. They were symbolic, however, of the new, cosmopolitan outlook of Oman.

Rapid change

The airports of the Gulf followed, for the most part, a similar pattern of development. First cleared as simple airstrips by the RAF in the early 1930s, they came into great demand by the 1960s and 1970s. All the Gulf states (not just those with old airstrips described here) created new international airports of their own in those decades. As the towns were also expanding at a very rapid pace, many of these airports had to be moved farther out, in search of space for the long runways needed for modern jet airliners.

The number of passengers using the airports of the Gulf annually was counted in millions by the 1990s. They were not, however, the only users of the airports. Air freight increased very rapidly in volume in the last decades of the century, reaching hundreds of thousands of tonnes a year, arriving at or passing through these airports. Dubai alone, the merchant hub of the Gulf, handled 250,000 tonnes of air cargo a year by the mid-1990s. New cargo terminals became just as essential as new passenger terminals had been a few years earlier.

H.M. King Hussein of Jordan piloting a Gulf Aviation Fokker Friendship on a state visit to Al Ain, Abu Dhabi Emirate, in 1966. Al Ain now has its own international airport.

The old Sharjah airport was the first in the UAE, and was used from 1932 until 1976, when the main picture was taken. The same scene in 1992 is shown as an inset.

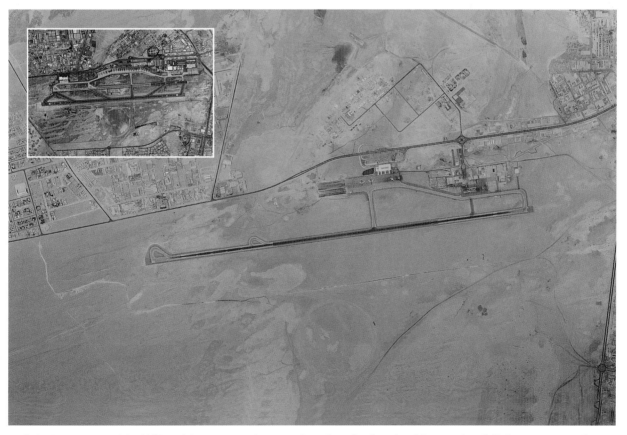

Dubai airport opened in 1960 and is now a major stopping place for long-haul international flights. Pictures taken in 1976 and 1994 record its rapid development.

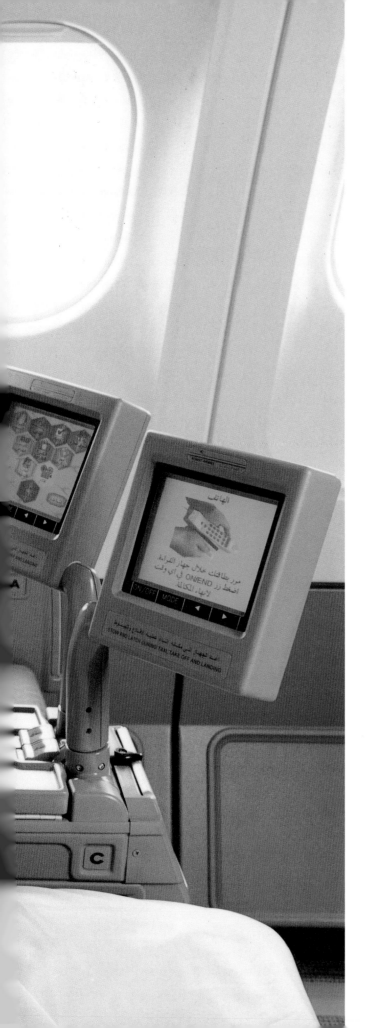

GULF AIRLINES

Until the end of World War II, all commercial flights in the Gulf were made by airlines from outside the region. After the war, however, Gulf states began to found their own airlines, just as European states had done immediately after World War I. The impulses which led to this development were similar in both cases too. Once again, ex-wartime planes were widely available, as were ex-wartime pilots to fly them. The peoples of the Gulf, moreover, had enjoyed half a dozen years of commercial aviation before the war, and their Rulers had been able to appreciate its advantages. After the war, the rapid development of the oil industry in all the Gulf states brought an unprecedented demand for aircraft in the region. The stage was set for the inauguration of locally owned airlines.

Saudia

The first civil airline to be launched in the Arabian peninsula was the Saudi Arabian airline, Saudia, which came into being at the end of the war in 1945. The airline was started by the gift of a Douglas DC3 Dakota from the President of the United States, Franklin D. Roosevelt, to King Abdul Aziz ibn Saud. Initially the airline concentrated entirely on domestic flights, linking the far-flung regions of this vast desert kingdom; these operations were started in 1947 with three DC3s.

Soon, however, Saudia sought the wider horizons and commercial opportunities of international flights; in 1964 the airline purchased three DC6s to provide a service within the Arab world, and improve facilities for pilgrims. The following year Saudia became the first airline in the Middle East to acquire

Gulf airlines offer the most sophisticated facilities to their passengers.

Douglas DC3 Dakotas were Saudia's earliest planes.

One of Saudia's A300-600s.

commercial jets, with the purchase of two Boeing 727s. By then its routes extended to Amman, Beirut, Cairo, Istanbul, Bombay and Karachi. The first jets were followed by Boeing 707s and Douglas DC9s. In 1967 Saudia became a member of the International Air Transport Association, IATA, and inaugurated its first flights into London's Heathrow Airport, with a once weekly service. This was soon upgraded to three times weekly and, indeed, London remains one of Saudia's main destinations abroad. The acquisition of Boeing 707s in 1968 enabled a non-stop, Jeddah-London service to be started.

By 1973 Saudia was carrying one million passengers a year on its flights, and two years later the airline introduced the wide-bodied Lockheed Tristar jumbo jets to its fleet. These were followed in 1981 by the large Boeing 747s, of which the airline had purchased ten by the year's end. By that time, one of Saudia's major operations was the transport of thousands of pilgrims for the annual pilgrimage to Mecca, the hajj.

Saudia opened an Aviation Technical Training Centre in Jeddah to train Saudi nationals in aircraft maintenance. Pilots and many other employees were also sent abroad for advanced training courses. So successful has been the company's training programme that by the mid-1990s over 75 percent of Saudia flight deck crews were Saudi nationals.

Airbus Industrie's planes first came into the fleet in 1984, with the purchase of 11 Airbus A300-600s. These were to be the major additions to carry the Saudia fleet into the early 1990s. By the middle of the decade Saudia was flying to 52 international destinations and 35 domestic ones, and carrying some 12.5 million passengers a year. The major elements of her fleet were 11 Airbus A300-600s, 23 Boeing 747s, 20 Boeing 737s, two Boeing 707s, 19 Lockheed Tristars, and one Douglas DC8.

Gulf Air

This Bahrain-based airline traces its origins back to 1950, and the arrival on the island of a former RAF pilot, Freddie Bosworth, who flew in with his old, ex-wartime, Avro Anson. More than 7,000 of these planes had been built during the war, when they were used for air-sea rescue and especially for training. They were already veteran aircraft, having first flown in 1935, and were based on a model built for Imperial Airways in 1933. The wings were of wood and the body had a steel tubular frame. Several of

Freddie Bosworth, founder of Gulf Aviation.

these planes had been delivered in sections to the RAF in Iraq in the last years of the war, and were assembled on the spot.

After the war, Bosworth had been travelling around the Gulf, looking for the chance to start a charter company to fly to places not on the BOAC scheduled route. So far he had not been successful. When he arrived in Bahrain he gave joyrides at 10 rupees a time (echoes of the earliest flight into Bahrain in 1929), and tried to found a flying club. Bahraini merchants were interested in the possibility of readily available flights and some of them, led by Husain Yateem and the Kanoo brothers, combined to finance the founding of Gulf Aviation in 1950.

The following year Freddie Bosworth flew back to England to purchase one of the versatile de Havilland Doves, to use on charter work for the oil companies. During a test flight in the Dove, he crashed and was killed. He is recalled in the novel *Round the Bend* by Nevil Shute (who as Nevil Shute Norway was himself a veteran aviator of both world wars and a leading figure in the aircraft industry); his principal character is said to bear a striking resemblance to the dedicated Freddie Bosworth.

This tragic accident put the fledgling company greatly at risk, but it was saved by BOAC who bought Bosworth's shares and became a major shareholder. BOAC also provided four Doves which, despite the accident, were to prove ideal aircraft for oil company work, flying passengers, mail and light supplies into remote desert airstrips. The increasing demands of the oil companies led to the expansion of Gulf Aviation, which acquired four de Havilland Herons in 1952, their first four-engined planes. These were followed in 1960 by four Douglas DC3 Dakotas, to supplement the original Doves.

A Gulf Air A320.

By the mid-1960s, Gulf Aviation was flying a regular daily service to all the Gulf states. During this decade three Fokker Friendships were added to the fleet as the workload increased with the eventual successes of the oil companies after many years of prospecting throughout the Gulf. Short Skyvans were bought in 1970 and used to transport 34 fat sections of pipe, projecting from the open freight door. Gulf Aviation also hired its first jet Trident aircraft from Kuwait Airways, and in 1970 purchased its own first jet aircraft, a BAC One-Eleven.

The major milestone in the airline's history came in 1974, when the Gulf states, Bahrain, Qatar, Oman and the UAE, combined together to buy the airline from BOAC, and its name was changed to Gulf Air. Its operations were increasing very rapidly with the boom in the local oil industry, and the number of employees in the company soared from 800 that year to 3,000 two years later.

Gulf Air concentrated on training nationals of the Gulf states to fill posts at all levels in the company. Local pilots are trained for two years in the USA and two years more in the Gulf before being accepted as fully qualified. Gulf nationals are also given advanced training as technicians, and by 1984 local engineers succeeded for the first time in completing a major overhaul of a Boeing 737. Since then the company has advanced rapidly in the field of maintenance, given priority by the founding in 1984 of the Gulf Air Maintenance Company in which Gulf Air and Abu Dhabi are partners.

By that year, Gulf Air had a fleet of four Vickers VC10s, three BAC One-Elevens, two Lockheed Tristars, and five Boeing 737s. At the beginning of the following decade the company became a member of IATA. Gulf Air's development increased rapidly during the 1980s also, and the company acquired its first long-haul Boeing 767 in 1988.

By its fortieth anniversary, in 1990, Gulf Air was carrying three million passengers a year. In the same year the company purchased its first Airbus A320, and in 1994 the first of six Airbus A340s. By then Gulf Air was carrying some five million passengers a year, and had ordered six Boeing 777s, carrying up to 350 passengers each. The company's profits increased rapidly, from around $25 million a year in the 1980s to some $47 million a year in the 1990s.

By the mid-1990s, Gulf Air's fleet consisted of 18 Boeing 767-300s, 14 Airbus A320-200s, four Airbus A340-300s (with an option of six more) and one Boeing 757F freighter, a total of 37 aircraft. The airline was flying to 51 destinations.

Modern Kuwait Airways aircraft.

Kuwait Airways

Kuwait Airways was founded back in 1954 by a group of local businessmen, as a small privately owned company with two Douglas DC3 Dakota aircraft. They flew from a rough landing strip with Nissen huts as the terminal. Initially there was a three times weekly service to Basra, and less often to Beirut. Services to Bahrain and Cairo were introduced two years later. This original company was known as the Kuwait National Airways Company; in 1956, however, it experienced financial difficulties (just as early European airlines had done) and the Kuwait government agreed a loan of £20,000 to double its capital, in exchange for 50 percent of the shares, and renaming of the company. So in 1957 this first airline became the Kuwait Airways Corporation. By 1962 Kuwait Airways was fully government owned.

The company now flourished, and developed rapidly along with the boom in Kuwait's economy. In 1962 the company bought Boeing 707s for intercontinental flights. In 1964 it acquired Trans Arabia Airways which for the past five years had been a dangerous competitor. That airline operated a service throughout the Middle East and to London. In 1968 Kuwait Airways bought their first Boeing 707. Ten years later the airline owned eight Boeing 707s, and had ordered four Boeing 727s and three Boeing 747 jumbo jets; the latter were delivered in 1978, the start of the company's wide-bodied operations. By then, Kuwait Airways was flying one million passengers a year. In the 1980s the company also acquired 11 Airbus A310 and A300-600 twin-engined airliners which were more economical on fuel than previous generations of the planes.

In 1990, along with the rest of the country, Kuwait Airways suffered a severe setback as a result of the Iraqi invasion of Kuwait. Fifteen of its aircraft were taken away to Iraq, including all the Airbuses, two Boeing 767s and one 727. Although some of these planes were returned much later, they needed extensive refurbishment.

However, Kuwait Airways worked rapidly to re-establish its fleet by leasing some aircraft and purchasing others, and by 1994 all its services had been resumed. By the mid-1990s, its fleet consisted of four Boeing 747s (three normal and one combi), five Airbus A300-605s, three A310-308s, three A320-212s, one A300-620 and one A340-313 with two more on order, as well as three 747-400s on order. One 747 and one 727 were being used exclusively as VIP aircraft. The airline by then was flying to 35 international destinations.

Emirates

Emirates airline was launched by the Government of Dubai, in October 1985, to encourage and boost commerce and tourism into the Emirate. From a modest start, operating with aircraft and pilots leased from PIA, and flying only to destinations in the Indian subcontinent, Emirates has experienced an extremely rapid expansion, and been greeted with enthusiastic awards by the travelling business community.

The first years of existence are difficult for any airline, and for Emirates they could have been particularly so. Initially the Iran-Iraq war hampered communications in the Gulf, and in 1991 the war for the liberation of Kuwait temporarily checked air travel there. The world recession, starting in the late 1980s, had further depressed air travel. Emirates had to be more than competitive to survive in this atmosphere, and from the start made superb service a priority.

An Emirates airliner being refuelled.

The route network was expanded in 1986 to include the Middle East and Western Asia, and in 1987 Emirates flew to London and Frankfurt. The Far East was the next region to which their planes began to fly.

Emirates soon built up its own fleet of Airbuses. Service within the planes continued to be a priority, and the airline was the first to introduce in 1992 a personal video for every seat in all classes throughout the plane. In the first and business classes, passengers are served in a fashion more reminiscent of the leisured days of Imperial Airways' Hannibals and Empire seaplanes. In Emirates, too, meals are presented on linen cloths laid with china (Royal Doulton in first class), and silver plated cutlery. By the mid-1990s Emirates' fleet consisted of six Airbus A300-600Rs, 10 Airbus A310-300s, with seven Boeing 777s on order for 1996. The airline was flying to 38 destinations around the world, and carrying more than two million passengers a year.

As an airline with such rapid growth, Emirates has recruited staff from all over the world. The airline is also making a firm effort to train Dubai nationals to fill appointments at all levels within the company, by providing advanced courses in commercial operations, aircraft maintenance and flight operations for local graduates at the Emirates/DNATA Training Centre. This Centre, built in the mid-1990s, has flight simulators for both Boeing and Airbus aircraft. Advanced students may also take an MSc course in aircraft maintenance at Cranfield in England and pilots graduate at the British Aerospace School at Prestwick in Scotland. Dubai Aviation College, founded in the early 1990s, is open to all students, and has courses in a range of subjects including air traffic control, basic engineering and foreign languages.

Qatar and Oman

Qatar and Oman both launched their own international airlines in 1993/94. Both countries had been partners in Gulf Air for the past 20 years, and Oman had long had a domestic airline, Oman Aviation. In the 1990s, however, air traffic in the Gulf was booming, and the success of the recently-founded Emirates was an encouraging example to follow.

Oman's international airline, Oman Air, was formed as a division of the long-established domestic airline, Oman Aviation, in 1993. By summer 1995 their international destinations comprised Dubai, Muscat, Kuwait, Colombo, Trivandrum, Karachi and Bombay.

Qatar Airways started operations in January 1994 with two leased aircraft, followed by four further aircraft at the end of the year. The airline expanded its route network very rapidly, adding two new destinations each month. By mid-1994 its planes were already serving 12 destinations, and by early 1995 they were flying to major airports in the Middle East, East Africa, South Asia and Europe, with Athens and London as their first destinations there.

Some of Emirates' fleet at Dubai International Airport.

AIRCRAFT OF

Douglas DC3-Dakota

First flown in 1935; by 1985 some 350 were still
in airline use world-wide.
Two air-cooled, radial piston engines.
Maximum cruising speed 200 mph at 5,000 feet.
Range with maximum load 352 miles.
Span 95 feet, length 64 feet 6 ins, height 17 feet.
Maximum number of passengers 32.

Boeing 747-200

First flight 1969.
Four turbofan jet engines.
Maximum cruising speed 588 mph at 35,000 feet.
Range with maximum load 7,126 miles.
Span 195 feet 8 ins, length 231 feet 10 ins, height
63 feet 5 ins.
Maximum number of passengers 516.

Boeing 757

First flight 1984.
Two turbofan jet engines.
Maximum cruising speed 585 mph at 31,000 feet.
Range with maximum load 3,684 miles.
Span 124 feet 10 ins, length 155 feet 3 ins, height 44
feet 6 ins.
Maximum number of passengers 239.

Boeing 767-200

First flight 1981.
Two turbofan jet engines.
Maximum cruising speed 560 mph at 39,000 feet.
Range with maximum load 2,888 miles.
Span 156 feet one in, length 159 feet 2 ins,
height 52 feet.
Maximum number of passengers 290.

THE GULF FLEETS

Airbus A300

First flight 1983; long-range version of the original
   Airbus A300.
Two turbofan jet engines.
Maximum cruising speed 556 mph.
Range with maximum load 2,680 miles.
Span 147 feet, length 177 feet 5 ins,
   height 54 feet 6 ins.
Maximum number of passengers 375.

Airbus A310

First flight 1983; long-range version.
Two turbofan jet engines.
Maximum cruising speed 560 mph at 35,000 feet.
Range with maximum load 4,344 miles.
Span 144 feet, length 153 feet, height 51 feet
   10 ins.
Maximum number of passengers 280.

Airbus A320

First flight 1987.
Two turbofan jet engines.
Maximum cruising speed 564 mph at 28,000 feet.
Range with maximum load 1,162 miles.
Span 111 feet 3 ins, length 123 feet 3 ins, height
   38 feet 7 ins.
Maximum number of passengers 179.

Airbus A340

First flight late 1980s; long-range variant of A330.
Four turbofan jet engines.
Range with maximum load 7,938 miles.
Span 190 feet, length 194 feet 10 ins,
   height 55 feet one in.
Maximum number of passengers 375.

AIR POWER

The first warplanes to appear in the Gulf were the RAF's old World War I biplanes, which were stationed in Iraq from 1921 onwards. They were soon to see active service defending the frontiers against raiding parties of Ikhwan bedouin from Saudi Arabia. King Abd al Aziz ibn Saud had forged these deeply religious bedouin troops to aid in the reconquest of his vast domain, but once that task was completed, he found their enthusiasm hard to contain.

When the powerful Ikhwan extended their raids into Iraqi and Kuwaiti territory, they were attacked by RAF planes. The desert offered no protection against bombs from the air, and although they did once manage to shoot down a plane by rifle fire, they were always forced to retreat. King Abd al Aziz realised that air power was something which traditionally armed bedouin could not fight, and forbade them to cross the borders.

By 1929 some of the northern bedouin tribes were in open revolt against their King, whose restraint they resented. They gathered together in the north to oppose him, but running short of grazing for their animals, crossed into Kuwait. The RAF ordered them to leave, or they would attack; King Abd al Aziz had moved north with his troops behind them. The bedouin fighters had hundreds of women and children with them. On the verge of starvation, they finally surrendered to Colonel Harold Dickson (the British official who signed the agreement for the Sharjah airport). As Dickson went out to meet their leaders, his car was mistakenly raked with machine-gun fire from the air – an early case of 'friendly fire', which in this case did no harm.

F15 fighter jets were some of the most important coalition aircraft in the Gulf War.

RAF Bristol fighters at Amman in the 1920s.

King Abd al Aziz was quick to appreciate the advantages of air power for Arabia, for patrolling his vast deserts and extremely long frontiers. In 1923 he formed a small air force and the British government presented him with several de Havilland DH9s. These two-seater bombers, flown by former RAF crews, were stationed in Tarut during the rebellion, presenting an additional threat to the rebel tribes. Soon this embryo Saudi air force was to acquire more planes, including four Westland Wapitis from Britain in 1931 and three planes donated by Italy in 1937. It was the first local air force to be established in the Arabian peninsula.

World War II and after

The storm of World War II scarcely reached the Gulf. The region suffered one air raid, carried out in October 1941 by a long-range Italian bomber flying from Eritrea. It dropped bombs on the oil refinery at Bahrain and oil facilities at Dhahran, but little damage was done. The need for vigilance was emphasised, however, and RAF planes flew from Muharraq, Sharjah and Masira in Oman, watching for enemy aircraft and submarines, mapmaking and carrying out aerial photography. Towards the end of the war, the Bahrain refinery was expanded "to provide

facilities for the production of aviation spirit," among other products.

The US government was also aware of the need to safeguard Saudi Arabia's vast reserves of oil, which prospecting in the late 1930s had hinted at. In 1944 they approached King Abd al Aziz seeking aviation rights in Saudi Arabia, and permission to build a military airport in Dhahran.

Permission was granted. The War Department jibed, however, at the $4 million costs, but their advisory committee on the Middle East recommended they go ahead with the base: "Although there is no immediate military interest, there is a long-range military interest in protecting the oil reserves, having a foothold in a strategic area, and having some military officers familiar with the area." The base was completed in early 1946, and under the agreement was to be run for three years by American military personnel, but would eventually be handed over to Saudi Arabia.

In the 1950s the RAF flew missions during the rebellion in Oman which centred on the almost impregnable Jebel Akhdar, and in 1959 the Sultan of Oman formed his own Omani air force. They were soon equipped with two-seater BAC Jet Provosts, and flew out of the difficult Bait al Falaj airfield.

In 1961 the RAF flew to Kuwait. In June of that year, Kuwait signed a Treaty of Friendship with

Great Britain, replacing the closer 1899 treaty, but her independence was immediately challenged by Iraq's President who declared that Kuwait was historically part of Iraq. It was not clear whether he intended to invade Kuwait to prove the point, but the British and Kuwaitis were uneasy, and on July 1 their Ruler requested British support. British troops were flown into Kuwait from Kenya on the same day. Others followed, flown in from Cyprus, Aden and the UK, using airfields all along the Gulf as staging posts. They were soon replaced by Arab League forces and the crisis defused.

Iran-Iraq War

Trouble flared again when Saddam Hussein, President of Iraq, invaded Iran in 1980. It was the start of a long conflict which risked involving neighbouring states, especially when their oil tankers and oil rigs were attacked by Iranian planes and gunboats. The long Saudi coastline was clearly vulnerable and was protected by Boeing AWACS (Airborne Warning And Control Systems) planes, constantly patrolling the skies. In June 1984 intruding Iranian planes were spotted in Saudi airspace; Saudi fighter jets scrambled and shot down two of the intruders. The Saudi air

force had shown its mettle and Iranian aircraft kept clear of its skies thereafter.

Air forces of the GCC states built up their own air power during the decade and by the end of it some were already a force to be reckoned with. Many of the pilots learnt their skills on the advanced Hawker Siddeley (BAe) Hawk jet trainers which, equipped with Sidewinder missiles, could also play a useful defence role. The Saudi Arabian Air Force, in particular, had some 42 McDonnell Douglas F15 Eagles, 44 Panavia Tornados, 100 older Northrop F5E Tiger fighter and ground attack aircraft, and five Boeing AWACS, supported by tankers, maritime reconnaissance planes and helicopters. Oman had a useful force of Jaguars and Tornados, and Bahrain had American F16s. The UAE and Qatar flew French Mirages, but these were more difficult to integrate into the joint action when the Gulf War started, because Iraq also flew Mirages; radar profiles could not distinguish between an Iraqi Mirage and a coalition one.

The danger of airpower to shipping was sharply demonstrated during the Iran-Iraq War when two Iraqi Mirages mistakenly fired Exocet missiles at the American frigate USS Stark, killing 37 of her crew and nearly sinking the ship. From then on,

Boeing E3 AWACS planes gave early warning of enemy aircraft in the Iran-Iraq and Gulf wars.

The Hawker Siddeley (BAe) Hawk advanced trainer was first used by the UAE in the Gulf region.

warships in the Gulf were on a state of permanent alert. This atmosphere of tension perhaps contributed to the tragic error made in the control room of USS Vincennes, in 1988, when the radar image of an Iranian airliner en route to Dubai was mistaken for an attacking warplane and the airliner was shot down. This episode finally convinced Ayatollah Khomeini of Iran to call an end to the war.

Gulf War

The peace that followed was brief. After disputes over oil production, Iraq invaded Kuwait on August 2 1990. Her massive army of a million men, the fourth largest in the world, rapidly overwhelmed its smaller neighbour, and moved on to the Saudi frontier. Iraqi troops were less than a day's drive away from the oilfields of Saudi Arabia's eastern province.

A coalition alliance of the GCC states, Syria, Egypt, Turkey, the USA, Britain, France, and Italy was rapidly forged. Their aim was to compel Saddam Hussein to withdraw his forces from Kuwait. The most pressing need, however, was to ensure the security of Saudi Arabia. King Fahd approved the deployment of American and other coalition forces on his territory. In all, 28 countries

sent military aid, but the main bulk of the military might was provided by the USA.

The American response was impressively rapid. Immediately the coalition was in place and King Fahd's agreement given, American fighters set out for Saudi Arabia. On August 7 the first 48 American fighters, F15C Eagles, arrived in Dhahran along with Boeing E3 AWACS Sentries. They had flown all the way from America.

This may not sound particularly impressive, in the days of airliners which regularly fly half way around the world, but the cockpit of a fighter plane is a very different matter. Fighter pilots normally fly missions of a few hours at most. They are strapped tightly to their seats, a helmet over their heads with a visor over the eyes, an oxygen mask fixed close across their face. Unable to move more than arms and feet, they set out on flights which took 14 to 17 hours and required 17 refuels, mostly in the air, on the way. Often they were alone in single-seater planes. They expected to be attacked on arrival by the overwhelmingly numerous Iraqi air force.

The build-up in that second week of August was quick, but the planes were still vulnerable. On August 8 the F16 Fighting Falcons arrived, powerful fighter and ground attack aircraft, and the following day F15E advanced Strike Eagles were at their base in Saudi Arabia. By August 11, 12 British Tornados were in Dhahran, and on the 13th British Jaguars and Nimrod surveillance planes arrived at Thumrait and Seeb in Oman. In 1987, the RAF had carried out a major air deployment exercise in the Gulf, called 'as Saif as Suriya' – 'Swift Sword'. It was to stand them in good stead now.

The Americans had been even more actively preparing the ground in the Gulf, during the threat of the Iran-Iraq war. Quietly they had upgraded and prepared military airbases in many of the Arab Gulf countries. In Oman they upgraded the airports of Seeb, Thumrait and Masirah, and more than trebled the length of the runway at the remote northern town of Khasab in the Musandam peninsula. In Saudi Arabia they had provided three new turnkey military airbases at Khamis Mushait, Taif and Tobuk, and in Bahrain they had built a new military airbase in the south of the island. All these bases were to prove invaluable.

The modern fighter and attack aircraft, for whom the bases had been prepared, were a very far cry from the flimsy biplanes seen in the 1920s, and even from the Spitfires and Hurricanes of the 1940s. These warplanes of the 1990s needed excellent runways and vast supplies of fuel. They were not only flying faster than the speed of sound (that is 762 mph at sea level, 660 mph at altitude), but most of them flew twice as fast. Their speed is now counted as Mach one (speed of sound), Mach two (twice the speed of sound), etc.

The biggest airlift

As the weeks went by the Americans transported a whole army with all its equipment, right across to the other side of the world. By November they had more than 200,000 men in Saudi Arabia. Then their commanding officer, General Norman Schwarzkopf, decided that he needed twice that number to achieve a sure and rapid victory: more men, more tanks, three more aircraft carriers and their accompanying battleships, to support the four carrier battle groups already in the region. So the airlift continued for another two months. It was not, of course, simply a matter of transporting men and their personal weapons. Each must be housed and fed for as long as he would be out

Lockheed's TR1 spyplane is an improved version of the U2, which saw long service with the US Air Force.

*Lockheed C5 Galaxies transported heavy equipment
and troops to Arabia over many months.*

there. He needed furniture and blankets, water to drink and for washing, air-conditioning during the summer months at least, transport, protective clothing against gas and chemical attacks.

The northern desert of Saudi Arabia offered none of these things. Even the Ikhwan bedouin, in the rebellion of the 1920s, found that when a thousand or so of them gathered together in the same place, with their sheep and camels, they soon ran out of food, and it was to avoid starvation that they crossed into Kuwait. Modern troops would need far more water, far more food, far more of everything than had those frugal bedouin.

The Americans had two huge types of carrier plane, Lockheed's C5 Galaxy and C141B Starlifter. These planes were capable of transporting tanks, vehicles and heavy equipment as well as men. But more was needed; old Lockheed C130 Hercules were pressed into service, and civil aircraft were chartered from the airlines. At the height of the airlift, 300 transport flights a day came into Saudi Arabia. Most came across the Atlantic, staging through Spain; some went the other way round the world, stopping to pick up marines in Hawaii.

The airlift kept the US forces' 89 Galaxies and 195 Starlifters constantly in operation. Crews did 20-hour shifts or worse; their impression of the airlift was one of constant fatigue. But their role was vital to the safety and wellbeing of the troops already in the desert; there could be no respite.

By the start of battle they had lifted 425,000 troops into northern Saudi Arabia. The Americans alone had 450 combat planes, 250 support aircraft and large numbers of helicopters, based on 30 airfields throughout the peninsula. Their vast aircraft carriers stationed in the Gulf were each the equivalent of another airbase. These ships were over 1,000 feet long, could carry up to 5,500 people each, as well as 100 planes and helicopters. They carried F14 Tomcat fighters, F/A18 Hornets, and older A6 Intruders as well as Apache and other helicopters. The Hornets, which had entered service only in 1984, accounted for two Iraqi MiG21s on one mission. A French aircraft carrier also in the Gulf carried 72 helicopters and 24 fighter planes.

An air war

On January 15 1991, the deadline ran out on the call for Iraq's withdrawal from Kuwait. The coalition approved the start of hostilities and in the night of January 16/17 the air attack began. If Kuwait was to be liberated at minimum cost of life, the Iraqi air force must be grounded and Iraq's radar, command and control systems and communications networks put out of action. These were the priority targets in the first days of the air war.

To ground the Iraqi air force, their airfields had to be put out of action. This task fell largely to the British Tornados which could fly in under the radar on attack missions, and release their cluster bombs from very low altitude. They were covered by fighters flying high above them, but had to fly through a devastating barrage of anti-aircraft artillery fire, which took a heavy toll: six Tornados were lost in action in the early weeks of the air war.

Meanwhile coalition fighter planes engaged the Iraqi air force in the skies. Iraq had hundreds of warplanes, including French Mirages and Russian MiGs and Su25s. After four days of fierce fighting, the Iraqi air force had been overwhelmed, and many of their planes fled to Iran. Although a few Iraqi planes would still take off, the coalition now had control of the skies. In the end, 37 Iraqi planes were shot down in air battles, almost all of them by F15 fighters. A Saudi air force pilot, flying an F15, shot down two Iraqi Mirages in one day.

High-tech warfare

Other coalition planes, such as the F16s, attacked radar sites, command headquarters, communication centres, nuclear and chemical plants, missile launch sites, and road bridges across the rivers. Raids on selected targets in the Iraqi capital were undertaken for the most part by the Lockheed F117 Nighthawk 'Stealth' fighters which had only recently come into action in the US air force. Designed to be almost invisible to enemy radar, they could place their bombs with such precision as to put them through a skylight or an air-conditioning shaft, as impressive film taken at the time showed.

Precision bombing was a feature of these aerial bombardments on selected targets. In this aerial war, bombs and missiles were laser guided, homing in on a dot of laser light aimed by the attacking aircraft or an accompanying plane. Or they could be guided by an electro-optical system fitted in the nose of the weapon, which seeks out a line of contrast, for instance a dark object on a light background. The pilot can direct such a weapon in flight, since he can see through a television data link just what it is seeing. A completely new guided missile system was the imaging infrared seeker. With this system, the

McDonnell Douglas' powerful AH64 Apache helicopter can also attack by night and in all weathers.

A camouflaged communications shelter in the Arabian desert.

weapon seeks the heat profile of vehicles and ships. The great advantage of the system was that once launched, the missile would guide itself and the pilot could fly off to safer skies.

The key to the success of these missions lay in the vast amount of information available to the pilots before setting out. This was collected by surveillance planes and satellites equipped with state-of-the-art reconnaissance equipment. Firstly three satellites, placed in orbits which collectively cover every country in the world, sent back a stream of images; one of them was nudged into an orbit that gave almost constant surveillance of Iraq and Kuwait. From 100 miles up, the satellites could easily identify vehicles, artillery, indeed any object over three feet long (no, they could not read car number plates), but one of them could continue observing through cloud or smoke haze.

Closer to home, Lockheed's U2 spyplanes and their updated TR1 successors patrolled the borders of Iraq and Kuwait, photographing far inside Iraqi territory. Boeing E3 AWACS planes (converted versions of the old Boeing 707s), with saucer-shaped radomes mounted above the fuselage,

were packed with sensitive radar and listening equipment. They could detect an Iraqi aircraft flying several hundred miles away, thus monitoring all movements and directing an attack on any enemy aircraft which took to the air.

Boeing 707s, equipped with side-looking airborne radar and a data processing centre, could spot a vehicle several hundred miles behind enemy lines and were a major help against Iraqi Scud missile sites. Finally, once the war started, Phantom reconnaissance planes, flying at more than twice the speed of sound (Mach 2+), took pre- and post-strike pictures, which were processed within a few minutes of the plane's return to base, so that the success of a strike could be immediately assessed.

Pilots themselves were able to work all round the clock, thanks to an ability to see in the dark. They wore night-vision goggles which electronically amplified the faint light of the moon and stars. Leading American fighters and attack aircraft were also equipped with forward-looking infrared systems which sensed the heat given off by tanks and vehicles for example, and produced a video picture.

Below the speed of sound

A number of veteran aircraft, using conventional weapons, could come into their own once the coalition had control of the skies, and Iraqi radar defences had been put out of action. Most famous of the old-guard planes were the almost 40-year-old, giant Boeing B52 heavy bombers, which were used to effect against the Republican Guard crack forces. These long-range bombers operated from Spain, Britain, and from the Indian Ocean island of Diego Garcia. Each plane carried 100,000 lbs of high explosives, enough to obliterate a substantial stretch of desert where Republican Guards were dug in.

The British brought out their 21-year-old Buccaneers towards the end of January, when aircraft with laser designation capability were needed to direct the medium-level bombing carried out by Tornados in the second phase of the air war. At this stage, too, the American Fairchild A10 Thunderbolt, commonly known as the Warthog because of its ungainly appearance, was able to operate successfully now the skies were clear of enemy threat. This relatively slow plane, with high manoeuvrability, was the great tank killer of the campaign, flying mostly at night. Despite its slowness, and operating at low altitudes, the Warthog was a good survivor largely because its two large engines, slung awkwardly along either side of the fuselage, have their infrared signature masked from heat-seeking missiles by the large and box-like tail surfaces. McDonnell Douglas Apache helicopters, naturally much slower than fixed wing planes but very powerful fighting machines and the most advanced of battlefield helicopters, were also successfully used for night attacks against enemy tanks.

One of the major targets of the campaign was the mobile launchers of Scud missiles, which the Iraqis used to worrying effect. Their mobility made them difficult to take out from the air, although satellite information could indicate the areas in which they operated. Special missions of American Delta Force commandos and British SAS units went behind enemy lines to destroy the sites, attacking them from the ground or pinpointing them with laser target designators for Warthogs to attack.

By the time the ground war started on February 23, the huge Iraqi army had been constantly attacked from the air for 38 days, and was in little state to fight. General Schwarzkopf had planned for this but of course he could not be sure what the

Setting up a Marine satellite system to transmit frontline pictures to the Pentagon.

situation would necessitate. He had demanded 60 days' supply of ammunition before he launched his attack. It was a cautious assessment. His battle plan involved a lightning strike encircling Kuwait and reaching into southern Iraq. Supplies to the rapidly advancing troops would be crucial. His planes had spotted hundreds of old dirt airstrips in the deserts of Kuwait and Iraq, made by oil prospecting parties. Fuel and ammunition for the tanks and armoured vehicles, and food for the troops were all flown up to the very front line, arriving on these desert airstrips sometimes before the troops did.

In the end, fighting on the ground was light and lasted a mere 100 hours, with casualties on the coalition side being minimal. Not surprisingly, many of the casualties were suffered by the coalition air forces, which together lost 75 planes, 42 in action and 33 in accidents. But the war had indeed been won in the air, as the original US air force chief of staff had forecast that it could be. He had been relieved of his post for talking too much, but his words were heeded. Above the deserts of Kuwait and Iraq, the coalition fought a war of the 21st century, against an opponent who had just been involved in a struggle more closely resembling World War I in style. Iraq possessed high-tech equipment too, but rarely had the chance to use it effectively.

FIGHTING AIRCRAFT

McDonnell Douglas F15 Eagle

Single-seater fighter, with two-seater version.
Two after-burning turbofan engines.
Most powerful fighter in the world.
Maximum speed Mach 2.5; combat radius
   580 miles.
Span 42 ft 10 ins; length 63 ft 9 ins.
First flight 1972.

General Dynamics F16 Fighting Falcon
(now made by Lockheed Martin)

Single-seater fighter and attack aircraft.
One after-burning turbofan engine.
Maximum speed Mach 2.05.
Span 31 ft; length 47 ft 8 ins.
First flight 1974.

General Dynamics F111
(now made by Lockheed Martin)

All weather attack aircraft.
Two after-burning turbofan engines.
First flight 1964.

Lockheed F117A Nighthawk 'Stealth' fighter

Single-seater attack aircraft.
Two turbofan engines.
Maximum speed Mach 0.9.
Span 43 ft 4 ins; length 65 ft 11 ins.
Range 1275 miles.
First flight 1981, developed in secret.
Flat angled surfaces deflect radar,
   coated in radar absorbent material.

OF THE GULF WAR

Boeing B52 Stratofortress bomber

Eight-engined heavy bomber, engines in four pairs.
Maximum speed 605 mph.
Span 185 ft; length 157 ft. Range 8,455 miles,
    service ceiling 46,000 ft.
First flight 1952.

McDonnell Douglas & British Aerospace AV8B Harrier

Single-seater air support fighter.
Maximum speed 660 mph.
Vertical take-off plane, much used on
    aircraft carriers.
Rapid deceleration to avoid enemy planes.
First flight 1978.

Panavia Tornado

Built by European consortium of British
    Aerospace, Messerschmitt-Bolkow-Blohm,
    and Aeritalia.
Two-seater multi-role combat aircraft.
Maximum speed Mach 2.1.
Span 45 ft 8 ins; length 54 ft 10 ins.
First flight 1974.

Fairchild A10 Thunderbolt 'Warthog'

Close support attack aircraft.
Maximum speed 730 mph.
Span 57 ft 6 ins; length 53 ft 4 ins.
Range radius 625 miles.
First flight 1972.

DUBAI
AIR SHOW

The Gulf now has its own aeroplane market in the shape of a massive, biennial air show, frequented by buyers from all over the Middle East. Dubai's International Aerospace Exhibition has rapidly expanded to become one of the largest air shows in the world, ranking third worldwide after the far longer-established shows of Farnborough in the UK, and Le Bourget in Paris. Access to the show is for professional visitors only and there are no open days for the general public.

The Dubai air show began in a much smaller way, as a forum for civil aircraft only; two shows of this kind were held in 1986 and 1988. HH Sheikh Mohammed bin Rashid Al Maktoum, Minister of Defence of the UAE, then proposed to expand the show to include military aircraft, which were also of great interest to the Gulf countries. In 1989 the first joint civil and military air show was organised. This greatly expanded show, held at Dubai's International Airport, attracted 10,000 visitors and was ranked fourth in the world after Farnborough, Paris and Singapore.

A further show of the same kind was planned for 1991 and a date at the end of January was agreed. It was not an ideal proposal. Cancellation of such a major event is never easy, but the organisers had no choice. Their chosen date coincided precisely with the air offensive preceding the liberation of Kuwait. They bowed to *force majeure* and postponed the show to November.

What must, at the time, have seemed far from the best of luck, in fact turned into a major boost for the air show. The vital importance of air power had been vividly demonstrated in the struggle for

Dubai's air show now ranks third in the world.

Visitors from all over the Middle East gather at the show.

Kuwait. Potential purchasers flocked to the show and the number of professional visitors doubled to 20,000. Manufacturers of aircraft and accessories were also now keenly aware of the Gulf region and its advantages as a market place; some 400 companies from all around the world brought their wares to the show, which that year included a wider field of land and sea defence as well.

Modern military aircraft, which had become household names during the conflict, were on display here. Visitors admired the sleek and manoeuvrable fighters speeding past at twice the speed of sound, and were impressed to be able to walk around the sinister-looking black Lockheed 'Stealth Fighter', even though this advanced-technology plane was not yet for sale in the region. In all, 57 planes were put on display, and 17 planes gave breathtaking air displays and fly-pasts.

The end of conflict in the Gulf region was celebrated also by commercial airlines, whose demand for modern airliners was increasing fast. The expansion of these airlines made Dubai an important market-place for the leading manufacturers. Smaller civil planes, of the private

and executive jets class, were also on display here.

The following show, held in 1993, built on the great success of the 1991 show and was able to attract an even larger clientele. 450 exhibitors and 25,000 professional visitors attended. By now the event was sufficiently well established to draw a number of VIP visitors, representing countries that clearly took the exhibition seriously. Prince Charles from Great Britain, Defence Ministers and heads of Civil Aviation Authorities from the Gulf States, the French Minister of Industry and External Commerce, the Defence Minister of Pakistan, and Indonesia's Minister of Research and Technology were among visitors attending the show.

It was a larger and even more spectacular show, with two huge display halls, 80 aircraft displayed on the ground and 30 giving flying displays. Generally rated the most dramatic of these displays were the tense, simulated dogfights undertaken by Russian fighter planes. Of the civil aircraft shown, the Airbus display of two giant planes, an A340 and an A330, flying together in a kind of massive aerial ballet was rated particularly impressive.

The world's most modern aircraft on display.

Success assured

This new International Aerospace Exhibition has leapt to world prominence for a number of reasons, the first of which is of course the region in which it is held. The Gulf is one of the most rapidly developing regions in the world, where business is still very buoyant. Commercial travel within the region, to and from the region, and transiting through the region, has expanded on all fronts. Dubai in particular, as the commercial centre of the Gulf, has experienced a massive increase in commercial passengers through its airport which was first opened only in 1960.

This great demand for air travel has brought a vast expansion of regional airline capacity, not only of the long-established airlines such as Saudia, Kuwait Airways and Gulf Air, but also of the newer and rapidly developing home-based airline, Emirates, and now the new international airlines of Oman and Qatar. Demand for airliners of all capacities has created an excellent market for the main contenders, Airbus Industrie, Boeing and McDonnell Douglas.

Military aircraft have enjoyed equal if not greater prominence in the region as a result of two major conflicts in little over a decade. All countries of the Arabian peninsula have seen the effectiveness of air power in the region, and have sought to equip their own air forces with up-to-date military planes. It has been estimated that some $60 billion was spent on defence in the Arab world in the few years preceding 1991, and that a further $65 billion will be spent in the coming decade. Much of this expenditure is devoted to air defence. Overall, the organisers of the Dubai show say that reports suggest that through the 1993 exhibition some $83 billion of business was concluded.

Despite the favourable environment, the show could not have attained its current international status as quickly as it has if the organisation had not been impeccable. The organisers have received tributes in the international professional press for this "exceptionally well run, well organised air show". One defence journal indeed concluded that "the efficiency of the Dubai show's organisation is also one of its main attributes". Professional visitors certainly appreciate the compact nature of the show's layout, and freedom from the hurly-burly of public open days.

With its own aircraft souq now firmly established in Dubai, and ultra-modern planes criss-crossing the skies, the Gulf has come a very long way indeed from those distant days when flimsy-looking biplanes established part of the longest air route in the world along its shores.

A Tornado on display at Dubai air show.

The Author

Shirley Kay first came to the Gulf in January 1968 and spent the next three years in Bahrain, Dubai and Muscat. During this time she often flew by Gulf Aviation (now Gulf Air), sometimes having the good fortune to visit the cockpit. She flew into the old Bait al Falaj airport near Muscat, and in a small plane to mud airstrips in the Wadi Semail and the top of the Jebel Akhdar.

She was again in Dubai, where her husband was British Consul-General, from early 1985 to autumn of 1990, and thus experienced the tension of the early weeks of the Gulf War and the rapid build-up of air power then. She watched these planes in action at the rapidly expanding Dubai air shows of 1989 and 1991.

Shirley Kay studied languages at Cambridge University, Arabic at Shemlan in Lebanon, and Middle Eastern archaeology at the Institute of Archaeology in London. This is her ninth book in the Arabian Heritage Series and sixteenth on the Middle East as a whole. It comes as a companion volume to *Seafarers of the Gulf.*

Bibliography

Dickson, H.R.P:
Kuwait and her Neighbours, 1956.

Dorr, R:
Desert Shield, 1991.

Fairbairn, T:
Action Stations Overseas, 1991.

Frater, A:
Beyond the Blue Horizon, 1986.

Henderson, E:
This Strange Eventful History, 1988.

Higham, R:
Britain's Imperial Airways, 1960.

Military History Magazine:
Desert Storm, 1991.

Rendall, I:
Reaching for the Skies, 1988.

Smith, Ross:
14,000 Miles Through the Air, 1922.

Thetford, O:
Royal Air Force, 1957.

Zahlan, R:
Origins of the United Arab Emirates, 1978.

Interesting articles in:

National Geographic, March 1921, May 1995.

Journal of the Royal Central Asian Society,
Vol. XX, April 2 1933.

The Aeroplane, Vol. 36, No. 8, 1929.

Imperial Gazette, 1929-1940
(especially Oct. 1932, Dec. 1934).

Air Pictorial, December 1994.

Flight International, April 5-11 1995.

ACKNOWLEDGEMENTS

Of the many people who have helped me trace the history of this section of one of the world's great air routes, I should especially like to thank Fred Humtley of British Airways Archives, Harry Fraser Mitchel of the Handley Page Association, Dennis Hanbury who flew HP42s and was in charge of oil company aviation after the war, Julian Lush, Alan Horan and John Wilkinson who all shared memories of the early days of oil company activity in the Gulf, Group Captain Ralph Cassels of the RAF, Ian Hope who helped guide my searches, and Michael Callister, Air BP's former Divisional Manager, Middle East whose enthusiasm for the history of flying gave the critical impetus to this book.

In the Gulf I would like to thank Abdulla bin Eisa al Serkal for lending his historic photographs of Imperial Airways aircraft, Lieutenant Commander David Samson, United States Military Attaché in Dubai, for his kind help in identifying military aircraft, Maurice Cregan and Michael Curtis for providing photographs, MAPS Geosystems of Sharjah for providing aerial photography, Nigel Perry and Damian James of Gulf, Hill and Knowlton for their assistance and support, and all the Gulf airports and airlines for supplying historic and modern photographs.

Above all I should like to thank Air BP whose sponsorship has made possible the publication of this book. I would particularly like to thank Glenn McBride, Air BP's Divisional Manager, Middle East, for his help and encouragement, and everyone at Air BP Dubai.

AIR BP

PICTURE CREDITS

Front cover: Ronald Codrai

Key:
L: Left; R: Right; B: Bottom; T: Top

Abu Dhabi Airport: 66
ADCO: 56
Airbus Industrie: 70, 72R, 73, 77 (all)
Al Serkal, Abdulla: 45B
ART video/Air BP: 30B, 75T
Bahrain Airport: 60, 61T
Boeing Corp: 74R, 76 (all except top)
Boeing Defense and Space Group: 81, 91
British Aerospace/Airbus: 37, 82, 91 (3rd)
British Airways: 23T, 42
Brooklands Museum: 8,
Brooklands Museum/Norman Pealing Ltd: 10
Cregan, Maurice: 67
Curtis, Michael: 5, 62, 68
Emirates airline: 75B
Fairchild Space and Defense: 91 (4th)
Fairs and Exhibitions: 92, 94, 95, 96, back cover
Havers, John: 55L, 72B

Horan, Alan: 55R
IPC: 48, 50
Jarrett, Philip: 12B, 12T, 13, 14, 15R, 16, 19, 31, 40, 80
Kay, Shirley: 17, 33, 61B, 64
Kuwait Airport: 59
Kuwait Airways: 74L
Lockheed-Martin: Contents page, 83, 84, 88, 89, 90 (all except top)
Lush, Julian: 46, 49, 51, 52, 54
MAPS Geosystems, Sharjah: 69
McDonnell Douglas Corp: 78, 86, 90T, 91 (2nd)
Middle East Centre Archives, St Antony's College, Oxford: 28, 32, 34, 58
Motivate Publishing/Adiseshan Shankar: 65
Oliver, John: 25B, 25T, 29, 35, 36, 44, 45T
Royal Air Force Museum: 9, 15L
Saudia: 72L, 76T
Science Photo Library: 6
Short Brothers: 41
Skeet, Ian: Title page
St John Armitage: 18
Sutton Library: 22, 23B
Sutton Library, British Airways: 30T
Vowles, Les: 20, 26, 38
Zandi, Dariush: 24

INDEX

THE ARABIAN HERITAGE SERIES

Arabian Profiles
edited by Ian Fairservice and Chuck Grieve

Land of the Emirates
by Shirley Kay

Enchanting Oman
by Shirley Kay

Bahrain – Island Heritage
by Shirley Kay

Kuwait – A New Beginning
by Gail Seery

Dubai – Gateway to the Gulf
edited by Ian Fairservice

Abu Dhabi – Garden City of the Gulf
by Peter Hellyer and Ian Fairservice

Sharjah – Heritage and Progress
by Shirley Kay

Fujairah – An Arabian Jewel
by Peter Hellyer

Portrait of Ras Al Khaimah
by Shirley Kay

Gulf Landscapes
by Elizabeth Collas and Andrew Taylor

Birds of the Southern Gulf
by Dave Robinson and Adrian Chapman

Falconry and Birds of Prey in the Gulf
by Dr David Remple and Christian Gross

The Living Desert
by Marycke Jongbloed

The Living Seas
by Frances Dipper and Tony Woodward

Mammals of the Southern Gulf
by Christian Gross

Seafarers of the Gulf
by Shirley Kay

Wings Over the Gulf
by Shirley Kay

Architectural Heritage of the Gulf
by Shirley Kay and Dariush Zandi

Emirates Archaeological Heritage
by Shirley Kay

Sketchbook Arabia
by Margaret Henderson

Juha – Last of the Errant Knights
by Mustapha Kamal,
translated by Jack Briggs

Storm Command
by General Sir Peter de la Billière

Looking for Trouble
by General Sir Peter de la Billière

This Strange Eventful History
by Edward Henderson

Travelling the Sands
by Andrew Taylor

Mother Without a Mask
by Patricia Holton

Zelzelah – A Woman Before Her Time
by Mariam Behnam

**The Oasis – Al Ain Memoirs of
'Doctora Latifa'**
by Gertrude Dyck

The Wink of the Mona Lisa
by Mohammad Al Murr,
translated by Jack Briggs

Fun in the Emirates
by Aisha Bowers and Leslie P Engelland

Fun in the Gulf
by Aisha Bowers and Leslie P Engelland

Premier Editions

A Day Above Oman
by John Nowell

A Day Above the Emirates
by John Nowell

Forts of Oman
by Walter Dinteman

Land of the Emirates
by Shirley Kay

Abu Dhabi – Garden City of the Gulf
edited by Ian Fairservice and Peter Hellyer

50 Great Curries of India
by Camellia Panjabi

The Thesiger Library

Written and photographed
by Wilfred Thesiger:

Arabian Sands

The Marsh Arabs

Desert, Marsh and Mountain

My Kenya Days

Visions of a Nomad

The Thesiger Collection
a catalogue of photographs
by Wilfred Thesiger

Thesiger's Return
by Peter Clark
with photographs by Wilfred Thesiger

Arabian Heritage Guides

**Off-Road in the Emirates
Volumes 1 & 2**
by Dariush Zandi

Off-Road in Oman
by Heiner Klein and Rebecca Brickson

Snorkelling and Diving in Oman
by Rod Salm and Robert Baldwin

The Green Guide to the Emirates
by Marycke Jongbloed

Beachcombers' Guide to the Gulf
by Tony Woodward

On Course in the Gulf
by Adrian Flaherty

Spoken Arabic – Step-by-Step
by John Kirkbright

Arabian Albums

Written and photographed
by Ronald Codrai:

Dubai – An Arabian Album

Abu Dhabi – An Arabian Album

**The North-East Shaikhdoms –
An Arabian Album**

Travels to Oman – An Arabian Album

MOTIVATE
PUBLISHING